The Dream Class

The Dream Class

Know Your Dreams, Know Yourself!

Patricia Ettinge

Veronica Lane Books

The Dream Class

by Patricia Eltinge

© 2024 First Edition

All photographs by Patricia Eltinge

All rights reserved. No part of this publication may be reproduced, stored in a retrieval system or transmitted in any form or by any means, electronic, mechanical, photocopying, recording or otherwise without the written permission by the Publisher.

ISBN 978-0-9992573-6-4

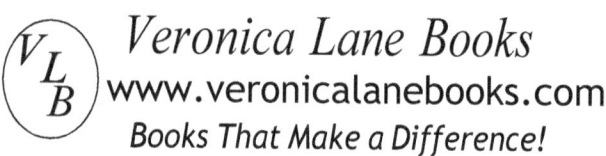

Veronica Lane Books
www.veronicalanebooks.com
Books That Make a Difference!

11420 US-1, Suite 124, N. Palm Beach, FL 33408 USA
Tel: +1(833)VLBOOKS +1(833)852-6657
email: etan@veronicalanebooks.com

Library of Congress Cataloging-In-Publication Data
    Eltinge, Patricia, 1949 –
    The Dream Class / by Patricia Eltinge
    2nd Edition
Library of Congress Control Number: 2018965113

Summary: An exploration of dreams and their meanings.

Acknowledgements

First and foremost, I acknowledge with much love Dr. Pat Allen, my mentor and friend for the past 28 years who has helped me through the rainy and difficult days, as well as celebrated with me the sunny and joyful times. I thank my generous and courageous friends and clients who have shared the precious treasures of their dreams in this book. I am grateful to my publisher and friend Etan Boritzer who guided me to the organized and artistic publication of this work. And finally, I acknowledge you the reader for your sincere efforts along the path of self-actualization.

Table of Contents

Foreward..i
Introduction..iii
1. What is a Dream?...1
2. Why Do We Dream?..4
3. Types of Dreams..8
4. Some Dream Terms..13
5. Yin Yang..19
6. Anima and Animus...22
7. How to Capture Your Dreams...26
8. What is a Dream Reading?...31
9. How to Read Dreams...33
10. Common Dream Themes..41
11. Dream Symbols..46
12. Common Dream Symbols...51
13. Colors..60
    Chakras as Color Symbols..62
    Black..71
    White...73
14. Numbers...75
15. Dream Case Studies..77
Final Thoughts..99
Recommended Books..100
Index...101

Foreward

At the time of the writing of this forward to Patricia's book, I am 84 years old. Patricia has been my student and even my friend for the past 25 years. It's important for me to tell these numbers because my legacy is important to me. I have anointed a few of my students to carry forth my teachings through their own practice and writings. Patricia Eltinge is one of my star students and extremely gifted in the esoteric area of dreams. I am very proud of this book she wrote that you are now holding in your hands.

All of us want to leave something valuable of ours behind for posterity. It's important that we come and go through this life and leave a positive inheritance for our children and our community. As a psychotherapist, teacher and mentor, my life has been about plumbing the depths of the individual and collective psyche. Dreams are the most important and effective way to get into our deepest secrets, our hidden traumas and our unseen behavioral patterns. Dreams give us insights into our destinies. Dreams are sacred tools for deep discoveries that every culture, since *homo sapiens* started walking the earth more than 200,000 years ago, has used. Today, with all of our technological advances and conveniences separating us more and more from our soul's journey, we urgently need to return to our dreams for guidance, inspiration and healing.

The *shamans* of old civilizations and those practicing even today, Sigmund Freud, Carl Jung, the Tibetan masters, pre-Columbian *naguals* and all the women and men who have been the vital link to our dreams continue to be acknowledged and studied by anyone interested in the vast possibilities of true human evolution. I am talking about evolution that includes the survival of our species, as well as the evolution each of us seeks consciously or unconsciously toward true happiness and true peace. Carl Jung called it the process of individuation whereby each of us manifests all the gifts and talents we have been bequeathed by our parents, our society and yes, by God.

Therefore, to find a book like Patricia's which endeavors the very difficult task of breaking down the inexact science and art of dream reading clearly showing the reader how to use the very original contributions which our teachings have brought to this field over the past 40 years, is indeed a great find. Understanding the *yin/yang* aspects of dreams and how they relate to the seemingly paradoxical *anima/animus* concepts that Jung developed, the color symbolism related to *chakras*, the hierarchical nature of dream symbols—these and other complexities have been explained simply and elegantly in Patricia's book.

I know this book will help countless sincere seekers of self-knowledge by showing how one can use dreams to know at the deepest levels what they want and what they don't want. Read the book slowly in order to digest all the wonderful material in it.

Pat Allen, Ph.D.
Carlsbad, CA
2019

Introduction

I remember a time when I was about six years old when my mother made a bubble bath for me and left me there in the tub to soak and play. I found myself sitting there, staring into the giant white mass of luminous bubbles in front of me. I noticed that this great heap I was immersed in was comprised of gazillions of individual bubbles that created a mountain of bubbles all around me. I just sat there in awe and experienced an aha moment. I thought, *Wow, am I just like that?* I almost stopped breathing while contemplating that existential concept. It was overwhelming. I further thought, *Maybe I'm just like that, a tiny bubble in a world of millions of bubbles around me.*

Not long afterward, my father took me to the beach in Santa Monica. I was playing in the sand, making my own abstract sand forms when another *aha moment* came over me. I remember stopping and just staring at all the sand spread out before me. I lifted a handful of sand up and then let the grains trickle out of my little hand. I carefully watched the stream of sand being released and cascading from my hand. As the sand poured, I thought to myself, *Where does it all come from and where does all go?* Again I questioned in wonder, *Am I as tiny as a grain of sand in the whole universe?*

During this period, I had a very traumatic early childhood experience that was repressed for many years. I was playing in our Los Angeles neighborhood when a young man stopped me and asked me to help him search for his lost puppy. Loving animals as I did, I believed him. He led me down a nearby deep drainage ditch that led toward a dark underpass. Once we were in the ditch, he took his penis out of his pants and tried to put it in my face. I said, "Yuk, that's where boys pee!" He turned me around, pressed me against the concrete wall of the ditch and started rubbing himself on my backside. I was not scared but rather in a super-heightened state of awareness at that moment. Suddenly, before he could do me any further harm, I clearly heard a voice from above call out my name several times. I shouted, "Oh, someone is here for me." The guy panicked, quickly pulled up his pants and ran away. After he ran away, I realized that there was no one else around and I did not know from where that voice had come. I was then alone wandering in this long, deep drainage ditch for some time as I could not climb out alone. Ultimately the police rescued me and took me home. I never told anyone what happened that day until I was an adult.

Soon after this traumatic incident, I recalled my earliest dream. This became a recurring dream. In the dream, I am trying to get away from an iconic old wicked witch who is trying to catch me. She is riding a broomstick but she can't fly very high. I am running away, staying just barely out of her reach. As I run away, I notice that I am able to fly higher but still just out of her reach.

I woke up and cried each time this dream recurred. Typically, I would run to my parents' bedroom and jump in bed next to my mother. I would tell her about the dream and she would try to comfort me by telling me that everything would be OK. She would lead me back to my room and say that she would leave the hall light on outside the room, with my bedroom door ajar. Years later, I understood that this dream pertained to that early childhood trauma and through my dream work I was finally able to process this ordeal.

I remember these early childhood incidents quite clearly, and I believe that these experiences led me to become a "seeker." By a seeker, I mean one who questions life's deepest mysteries and who is willing to go on any quest to find answers. I would say that because no adults could give me guidance in these early and very profound existential matters, I was motivated to start finding answers on my own.

After attending the University of Southern California, I pursued professional careers in fine arts, theatre, film, TV and modeling. During that time, I also indulged in the hedonistic worlds of New York, Hollywood and Paris. However, because I always retained a certain high idealism, I only found parts of the larger puzzle I was trying to piece together. I remember a vivid dream from this formative time of my life.

I dreamt a girlfriend and I were visiting a rustic beach house. There were different rooms in the house, and in each room there were unique and exotic items of clothing for sale. The men and women who lived in the house communally all seemed very mellow and welcoming. They were living an alternative lifestyle and looked happy and healthy. They offered us some exotic and unusual teas.

The rustic house, the hippy people and the different rooms represented new and different options. The clothes represent *persona*, meaning how we present ourself in the everyday world. I took the dream to mean that I was moving out of my hedonistic lifestyle to a more earthy and meaningful life which I soon thereafter did.

Then, already in my early 30's, I met and married a now world-famous holistic doctor. Together we founded a successful herbal medicinal products company and holistic health clinic. During this time, I became a Master Herbalist and a Certified Iridologist while simultaneously studying various other alternative healing arts. I started to see my path more clearly as a healer. I discovered my abilities to empower others to strive for their own health and wellness. I came to realize during this period that my life's work was not only to dispense healing herbs or to put my clients on a great healing program but also to teach them to see their life from a new perspective. I understood during this time that healing starts with a change of perception.

I was becoming more and more confident in my abilities as a healer. However, as each of you readers knows, life often throws us a big, unexpected curveball. For a period of two years, my life imploded with great force. A litany of tragedies befell me. I suffered two very difficult miscarriages. Alongside our very demanding natural healing business, I was also raising and training show horses. Our finances took a deep dive and death visited my family. My father, mother, and brother died from various tragic illnesses in this short period of time. I also discovered that there was infidelity in my marriage.

During this tumultuous chapter of my life, I had a powerful dream that I could not disregard. Actually, it's called a precognitive dream, a topic I will discuss in more detail further in the book. I was sound asleep when I abruptly heard my name called out in the same manner as I heard when I was kidnapped as a child. I distinctly heard a forceful voice yell out, "Patricia, Patricia!" I awoke and sat straight up in bed. This was a startling wake-up call. I knew then and there that my husband and I had to part ways, and that I needed to steer the course of my life in an entirely new direction. I started to get an inkling as to how dreams and waking life are closely related.

My life eventually evolved into a new phase of exploration and learning. A friend took me to see Dr. Pat Allen at a seminar in Los Angeles. I immediately connected with her energy and loved her irreverent wit and intellect. I loved the way she was able to deliver a barrage of scientific information with her own twist of humor. Dr. Allen's wealth of knowledge was definitely more than I could comprehend at the time but I knew that she had something I needed to learn and that I wanted to study with her.

During the ensuing years, I found that when Pat appeared in my dreams, it not only corroborated our close teacher/student relationship but that those dreams also helped me to start believing in my own inner wisdom. I started studying psychology with Dr. Allen at her private Los Angeles groups and at The WANT® Institute in Orange County, where she is the Director. The Institute became my sanctuary, a well of crucial life information that I never had access to before meeting this wonderful teacher. The gold mine of infinite possibilities that opened pulled me deeper into the wellness sciences. I began to see the connectivity between ancient wisdom and modern thought. My background in the arts allowed the dream work that I was studying at that time to uncover hidden facets within myself.

At this time I was also trying to salvage what was left of my business, manage my property, having to let go of my beloved horses and basically trying to regroup my life. I had dreams with very masculine images of motorcycles, horses, planes and tall buildings. I recall a specific dream from this phase of my personal growth. I was in my living room observing a cat on a couch. It was panting and looked like it was dehydrated and dying.

My dream readings during this stage of my studies really opened my eyes to the fact that I was operating with an out-of-balance, self-destructive masculine (*yang*) energy. The reading of the cat dream showed that my feminine (*yin*) side was being neglected. This work inspired me to systemically dump all of the old, distressing parts of my previous incarnation. My dreams from this period further inspired me to go deeper into dreams and dream analysis. I realized that I had found the box with the missing pieces of the philosophical conundrums that my childhood imagination could not put together. In my continuing education process, I knew that I wanted to go on sharing my discoveries and gifts with others.

II

Imagine you are walking on a beach and you find a bottle. You open the bottle and discover a note in it. However, the note is written in Cyrillic Greek script. This is what a dream is like. We receive a message from the container of our minds but it is written in a foreign language, the language of symbols. If you want to know the meaning of the note, you must take it to an interpreter who has the ability and the experience to give you a meaningful translation of the note. However, in a dream reading only you can understand the personal connection to the note in the bottle.

I wrote this book in order to empower others to own what is in their unconscious, the realm of repressed or denied personal and universal truths. Learning the tools needed to read a dream allows one to associate the deeper meanings of the symbolic messages that we receive during sleep in order to ascertain how our psyche is perceiving our daily life. The goal of this work is to help you readers become fully actualized human beings; that is, to grow toward the fulfillment of one's own meaning in life.

Why the title *The Dream Class*? I wanted to create a primer that anyone can use to teach oneself the basics for reading that mysterious message in the bottle. My hope is that you the reader will feel drawn to explore, individually or in groups, these wondrous realms not only for your beneficial utilitarian purposes but also just for the sheer joy of allowing yourself to go on these otherworldly expeditions.

Patricia Eltinge
Los Angeles, CA
2019

1. What is a Dream?

Dreams get us closer to our wounds. Courage flourishes at the wound.
— Dr. Pat Allen

Dreams seem to come from a different dimension and they speak a language all their own. Dreams act as bridges between the lower and upper worlds, between the unconscious and conscious mind. A dream is generally a crystallization of our unconscious mind working with experiences, images and impressions from our daily life. It is important to uncover the dreamer's present conscious situation since the unconscious is always in sync with the conscious activity of the moment.

Dreams are very useful tools for self-discovery and problem-solving. A dream is a coded version of the inner workings of our mind, reflecting how we really perceive what is going on in our personal life. By 'coded' we mean that dreams talk to us in symbols as we are not always ready to look directly at some hidden truths that exist in our waking state. The language of the dreaming mind is primarily that of a picture metaphor. The symbol or dream image is a visual representation of the dreamer's inner associations, memories and feelings that created the image. As Carl Jung put it, the unconscious aspect of any conscious event is revealed to us in dreams where it appears not as a rational thought but as a symbolic image, an emotionally charged pictorial language.

Our unconscious mind speaks to us through symbolic images so that we can allow ourself to look more deeply into that which may be distasteful in our waking state. In what we call nightmares, the unconscious mind speaks to us in stronger symbols indicating that we need to take a more urgent look at some issue in our life. However, it is very important to remember: *There are no bad dreams!* There may be scary images but each dream, whether it is seemingly pleasant or unpleasant, has a purpose that is worth deeper study.

So, we look at a dream and study it in order to understand how the unconscious views our life, not just how it appears in our everyday awareness. In simple terms, we have experiences in our daily life that are pleasurable, painful or neutral. The dream is the mind reflecting deeply and honestly on those experiences or to ready us for new ones.

We know that dreaming occurs during most stages of sleep. The dreaming which occurs during the rapid eye movement (REM) sleep cycle promotes creativity and creative problem-solving and is typically experienced in the last two hours of sleep. However, we also dream during the stages of sleep called NREM (N3 and N2). REM dreaming is a time when new information is integrated into older data, and novel or symbolic connections between the old and new are built, allowing new solutions to emerge. During deep sleep, the glymphatic system activates, allowing the brain to clear out toxins, including harmful proteins linked to brain disorders such as Alzheimer's disease.

Psychologically, when "we sleep on it" certain dreams help us with emotional brain processing which seems to take the pain out of difficult or even traumatic emotional experiences. You can think of dreaming as an emotional convalescence, helping the dreamer to feel better about stressful or hurtful experiences.

Dreams may come from many sources, from the body itself (including the various parts of the composite brain) and the stimulated senses, from emotions and from all kinds of conscious and unconscious reactions to things, from attempts to psychologically digest past events, and from apprehensions and musings about future events. Dreams can emanate solely from one's own personal unconscious as well as from the collective unconscious. In Western societies dreams have been relegated to the province of psychoanalysts seeking to unlock the doors of personal neurosis and psychosis. However, in most cultures present and past, dreams have been treasured as gifts from the entire universal store of mysteries and revelations.

Dreams have their own wisdom and can point to missing aspects in our life that have resulted from a lack of perception in a waking life situation or from an unrecognized psychological state. The dream may simply provide us with more details pertaining to a specific life issue. It makes us pay attention to areas of reality that our conscious mind resists looking into, thereby allowing us to become aware of areas where we need to pay more precise attention.

2. Why Do We Dream?

To Awaken Insights

We awaken insights through our *instinct*, which is our feminine, feeling *yin* side. One may dream that they are going down some stairs, down a road, down into a cave, into a basement, or underground. This kind of dream gets us in touch with our instinctive side that gives us insights into how we truly *feel* about people, situations and things in our life.

We also awaken insights through our *intuition*, which is our masculine, thinking and doing *yang* side. You may dream that you are going up; that is, up a road, up in a plane, up a mountain, or up a tall building. This kind of dream gets us in touch with our intuition which are insights into how we *think* about people, situations and things.

To Enhance the Quality of Our Life

We may be dealing with a health issue, personally or with someone we know. By becoming more in touch with the inner workings of our mind through our dreams, we become more in touch with physical wellness matters that may be concerning us in our waking life. A dream may help us to know how best to handle the quality of our physical wellness.

In our professional or work aspects of life, a dream can get us in touch with how to qualitatively improve those areas. For example, John dreams that he is at the helm of his sailboat with his crew, adjusting his course on an ocean voyage. The

next moment John's sailboat is moving down a busy highway with a low bridge ahead. If they continue on this course, he realizes that the mast will surely break off and ruin the boat. Due to in depth examination, John realizes that if he and his business partners continue on the current course they are pursuing a particular business deal, it will be a disaster for the company.

To Gauge Our Relationships

Dreams with water images i.e. oceans, lakes, ponds, puddles, showers, pools, and all forms of water including rain, snow, ice, and even mud indicate the level of commitment or emotional involvement in our relationships. For example, if a dream is dealing with a relationship issue, a frozen pond might reflect being stuck in a relationship, or even being stuck in one's sensuality. Whereas, floating blissfully in a warm tropical lagoon can reflect our blissful immersion in a sensuous relationship. Dreams like these help us look into specific areas to see where we want to make changes, or if we are happy with the status quo i.e. being in our comfort zone.

To Establish Emotional Stability within Oneself

Our modern life is oftentimes filled with emotional volatility, and dreams focus on the emotional impact of those experiences and circumstances. The limbic system which processes emotional memories is found to be one of the most active areas of the brain during REM sleep. Dreams that represent extreme emotional content such as fear, anger, or hate are a source of insight for our personal growth and development, indicating stability or instability within ourself. These dreams benefit us as a step for personal healing. Even if our mind is producing emotionally-charged dream images, sometimes also called nightmares, these dreams act as mirrors of our emotional states, creating a tableau that helps us to choose how we want to handle these types of things.

Dreams where people or things die or violent dreams where shooting, hacking and slashing occur might be scary but are purposeful messages from the unconscious. Whenever there are death images involved in a dream, they are indicating that there are aspects of oneself that one may no longer need. So, one can gain emotional stability by facing these intense aspects within oneself, such as old behaviors and attitudes that can be released from our waking life.

One may dream that they are sick or in an accident. One may dream that they are killing someone in a dream. That does not mean that the dreamer is psychotic and may cause others harm. This type of violent dream can mean the dreamer is ready to let go of unnecessary thoughts, feelings or behaviors. This kind of dream points to something that you are ready to finish working out in your waking life, such as an unresolved hurt feeling or unfinished business.

Or you may dream that you have great physical ability and wellness with terrific mental acumen and you are totally enjoying life, indicating a positive emotional state. Those dreams typically don't happen during times of personal growth but they do indicate that you have come to some measure of stability.

To Relieve Stress and Anxiety

You may be experiencing personal anxiety or stress about yourself, or loved ones. A recovering addict may dream of using drugs, drinking, sex or overeating, etc. These dreams of indulgence in a person's addictions will often help to desensitize the dreamer to their fear of sobriety. Such dreams provide a *free party*, so to speak, for the dreamer although it does not mean that the addict is really going to *fall off the wagon*. The dream can actually relieve the person, kind of a pressure valve to help them adjust to the stress and anxiety of sobriety in their waking life.

There are dreams that relate to performance anxiety whether it is in sports, business or in the bedroom. For example, if a dreamer is in a runaway car where the brakes have failed that indicates that the dreamer does not feel in control of some aspect of their life. The anxiety in the dream calls for the dreamer to examine what areas in their life they need to address that are out of balance. Once fully examined, the dreamer may find some relief from that situation, person or thing that is causing them anxiety by knowing what area needs to be worked on in their waking life.

All dreams wish us well.
– Dr. Pat Allen

3. Types of Dreams

Daily-Life Dreams

You could be experiencing a difficult situation at work, whether it is a deadline, a relationship issue with a co-worker or a manager, or some dissatisfaction with the job itself. In your dream, you see yourself driving in a car with an unruly passenger up a bumpy, unsafe mountain road. Perhaps in your daily life, you are suppressing or trying to put aside that work situation and carry on normally but your dream is alerting you to a deeper, more troubling aspect of this situation.

You might be telling yourself and your friends that you'd like to be in a relationship. In a dream, you see yourself sitting alone on a beautiful beach, wanting to jump into the inviting turquoise water but not allowing yourself to get up and go into the water. You could be starting a new relationship with some trepidation in your waking life. Perhaps you dream that it is a cloudy day and you are out on the ocean on a paddle board. Suddenly you see a giant wave coming at you from far out on the horizon. You begin to paddle fast toward the shore, fearing that the wave may overwhelm you and cause a major mishap. Daily life dreams address situations whether or not you are consciously dealing with them.

Dreams about the Past

Dreams can be coded reflections of not just the recent past (daily events) but dreams can also reflect our unconscious, unresolved issues relating to the

distant past, e.g. our childhood, teen or young adult life. We often have recurring dreams. These usually point to a significant issue in your life that has not yet been resolved.

Being chased by a monster can represent an old idea, thought or feeling that is nagging you and that you don't agree with, or that you don't want in your life. Maybe you were molested as a child and still have traumatic feelings about that event and some old ogre is chasing you in a dream.

You might see images of an old rocking chair in your dream, perhaps a rocking horse that reminds you of a time when you felt playful and safe. These images could signify some parts of your upbringing or childhood that you liked and may want to keep.

Prophetic Dreams

Prophetic or predictive dreams are rare. These dreams are also referred to as precognitive dreams, a form of extra-sensory perception (ESP) in which a person perceives information about places or events in the future through paranormal means before they actually happen. However, you can never tell if a dream is prophetic until after the fact.

These types of dreams can take place in ordinary settings or even in science fiction or futuristic places. Prophetic dreams read much differently than ordinary types of dreams. They can arouse the dreamer to a state of emotional urgency and unease, or just a state of knowing. These dreams can be personal or they can be about an event or a situation that involves others. The premonition dream is the psyche's way of preparing the dreamer for some potential inevitability.

However, as noted, these dreams are extremely rare. Be aware that, for example, that if one has a dream where a relative dies, this oftentimes represents some aspect of the dreamer or their own behavior that no longer serves them and that they are ready to release.

Memory Consolidation and Pruning Dreams

Dreams are a means by which our minds perform both memory consolidation and memory pruning. The mind decides what experiences, teachings, emotions, etc. are worth remembering and what items are superfluous or useless to its owner's well-being.

For example, you might dream that you are in an ancient redwood forest and loggers are cutting down trees. You notice that one wonderful, majestic tree has been left standing, showing you that there is some ancient wisdom worth keeping as your own. That may also indicate that there is something important you need to recall and let other matters be released.

In another dream, something or someone dies. Depending if it is a masculine or feminine image, you can reflect on which people, things, thoughts or feelings are no longer necessary in your life, or that you are ready to release.

Trauma Dreams

There are dreams wherein the dreamer is reliving an event that produced an emotional or physical trauma in their life, such as an experience that occurred during wartime or from a physical assault. This type of dream often repeats itself and becomes quite disturbing. Note that a trauma can be relived in a dream without references to the original trauma but symbolic images may be used by the unconscious to reference the trauma.

Through working with a dream reader, the dreamer can gradually desensitize to the trauma by talking about how they are feeling in the dream. Talking about these difficult dreams helps one to connect the dots, or better understand how the mind and body are interconnected and affect one another due to the trauma. Helping to give the dreamer an understanding of this process by which the body and mind connect to relive a trauma in the dream, helps the dreamer to get a measure of awareness and control over their reactions in both the dream state and the waking state, and also helps eventually to take the sting out of those traumas. We must "Push the arrow through" so to speak. This method of dealing with trauma is preferable to "pulling the arrow out."

Also, patience and sensitive emotional support on the part of loved ones and/or a therapist can make the relived trauma somewhat bearable until the dreamer is able to start neutralizing the trauma out of their psyche.

Lucid Dreams

A lucid dream is a vivid dream during which the dreamer is actually aware that they are dreaming as if they are watching a movie. During a lucid dream, the dreamer may be able to have some influence over the dream characters, narrative, and environment. Lucidity occurs when certain areas of the brain that are normally inactive begin to activate resulting in a heightened degree of self-reflection and consciousness within the dream. It is often considered a state where the ego (dream-self) and the unconscious self (represented by dream characters and archetypal imagery) can interact and dialog directly. For example, sufferers of nightmares like children or PTSD victims have benefited from the ability to become aware that they are indeed dreaming and not in a real-life situation, thereby gaining therapeutic benefits. Achieving lucid dreaming awareness helps the dreamer to be able to change their actions in the course of the dream. This ability can help them to mitigate their symptoms. Some experienced lucid dreamers have learned to use dreams for specific practical goals such as atheletes, artists looking for inspiration, or computer programmers looking for a screen with their desired code.

Note: In our system of dream reading, we encourage the dreamer to allow the unconscious to express itself freely. In this way there is a natural and progressive personal growth that can arise from our dreams. If we find ourself aware that we are dreaming, a benefit can come to us when we put aside the urge to control the dream but rather trust our unconscious to be an aid to consciousness. Know that there is an unconscious wisdom within the dream that guides the dreamer to ask profound questions. With this integrated approach to lucid dreaming we start to lose the anxious reactions that scary images bring up in dreams and learn to trust the unconscious as a source of wisdom. As we develop our abilities to better capture dreams, a certain lucidity develops naturally in the dreamer.

4. Some Dream Terms

These are dream terms that we employ, and are useful in our reading of dreams. The simplification and the distillation of these terms allows the layperson to get an easier comprehension of our work, rather than having to delve deeply into classic psychological theories. By having a grasp of the terms, you will become more fluent and benefit more fully from your dream reading practice.

Analytical psychology

School of psychotherapy, pioneered by Carl Jung, emphasizing the importance of the individual psyche and the personal quest for wholeness or integration of the conscious and unconscious mind.

Anima

A term introduced by psychologist Carl Jung connoting the feminine part of a man's personality. Anima is the feminine word for soul, derived from Latin.

Animus

Also introduced by Carl Jung connoting the masculine part of a woman's personality. Animus is the masculine word for soul, derived from Latin.

Archetype

A term coined by Carl Jung that represents the general essence of a person, animal or thing as a symbol or motif taken from literature, art, or mythology.

Androgynous

The male and female energies accessed within oneself.

Androgynous Semantic Realignment (ASR)

A system developed by Dr. Pat Allen using communication tools to change people's everyday linguistic habits in order to facilitate a holistic integration of the conscious and unconscious mind.

Collective Unconscious

The part of the psyche that is independent of the ego and personal conscious mind and that originates from our human evolution, the contents of which are instinctive and archetypal in nature.

Consciousness

A state in which one is aware of the processes and the elements of the mind and body, as well as external circumstances.

Desensitization

The process in dreams that helps diminish emotional responses to negative or positive stimuli in our life through incremental exposure to them.

Ego

One's sense of personal identity or the Self, consisting of the will and the mind, with a priority of taking care of the body.

Ego-dystonic

Denoting aspects of a person's thoughts, feelings, impulses, attitudes, and behavior that are inconsistent with the rest of their personality or self-concept, particularly with their gender identity.

Ego-syntonic

Denoting aspects of a person's thoughts, feelings, impulses, attitudes, and behavior that are consistent with the rest of their personality or self-concept, particularly with their gender identity.

Individuation

A term introduced by psychologist Carl Jung representing a life-long process of transformation whereby one becomes fully integrated with all of one's potentials.

Instinct

The innate experiential feminine process of physiological and temperamental behavioral response or sensation to external stimuli through feelings.

Intuition

The innate masculine ability to understand something immediately by the extrapolation of intellectual data beyond conscious awareness through mental processes.

Life Script

A term coined by psychologist Eric Berne referring to an individual's life story that is developed by age four, and that is usually maintained throughout one's life as patterns of thoughts, feelings and behavior.

Limen

The threshold of consciousness between sleeping and waking, lasting three to four minutes.

Metaphor

An image or symbol that represents a personally meaningful picture of a complex cluster of memories, feelings, ideas or experiences that points to an issue the dream is attempting to resolve.

Myths (aka fairy tales and folklore)

The universal archetypal stories encountered and used by human beings from time immemorial as moral lessons.

Persona

The outward projection of one's self that an individual presents to others.

Psyche

The totality of all psychological processes, both conscious and unconscious, the entirety of the Self.

Psychoanalysis

A method pioneered by Sigmund Freud for the purpose of making a detailed examination of the elements of the mind, typically as a basis for discussion or interpretation.

Rational Decision Making

A process used in Androgynous Semantic Realignment that helps an individual choose alternatives to reactive behaviors.

Repression

The process of unconsciously hiding feelings, desires or impulses that occur typically before the age of three and can remain hidden in the unconscious.

Self

The Self (capital S) represents the entire psyche, the unified totality of the unconscious and conscious of an individual.

Self-actualization

A term coined by psychologist Abraham Maslow representing the growth of an individual toward fulfillment of their highest potential in life.

Shadow

Coined by Carl Jung, the shadow or dark side is the unknown, repressed or denied side of the personality.

Subconscious

The part of the mind of which one is not fully aware but which influences one's feelings and actions. A sort filter between the conscious and the unconscious.

Suppression

The act of consciously stopping oneself from expressing feelings, desires or impulses.

Symbol

The language of dreams is conveyed as symbols; that is, an object or image that appears in dreams representing unconscious thoughts or feelings.

Syndrome

A group of symptoms that operates together and are characteristic of a specific disorder.

Transactional Analysis

A therapy developed by Eric Berne utilizing the meaning behind words in order to help people negotiate with, rather than intimidate or seduce others.

Unconscious

The part of the mind of which one is not fully aware but which influences one's feelings and actions, the most hidden part.

Yin Yang

Complementary forces of the universe. Yin represents feminine energy. Yang represents male energy.

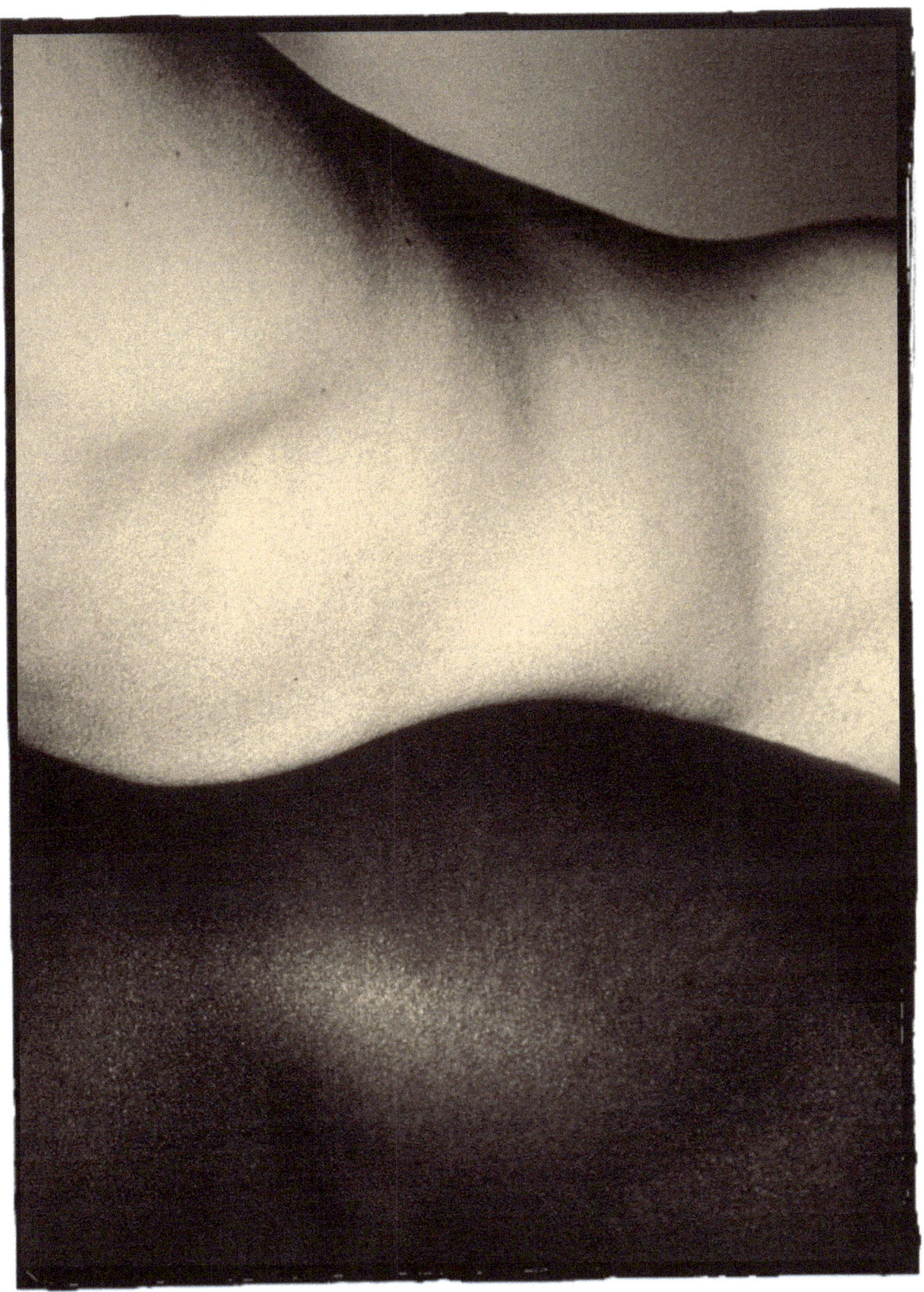

5. Yin Yang

Before getting into dream symbols, their more specific meanings and how to read those meanings personally in order to get the many benefits from dream reading, it is important that we review and understand one of the most important underlying tenets of our system—Yin and Yang. In our teachings, Yin represents the female attributes related to being patient, receptive and vulnerable. Yang represents the male attributes of being able to compete, conquer and control.

In Chinese philosophy, yin and yang (*yīn/yáng*) literally means "dark-bright" or "negative-positive." Yin and yang describe how seemingly opposite or contrary forces (dualities) may actually be complementary, interconnected, and interdependent in the natural world. Also, we start to see how yin and yang give rise to each other and how they interrelate with one another in a holistic way.

Yin and yang may be viewed as the binary language of the universe. Tangible dualities are thought of as physical manifestations symbolized by yin and yang. Examples of these dualities (in yin-yang order) are night and day, female and male, cold and hot, soft and hard, moon and sun, water and fire, alkaline and acid, matter and energy, negative and positive, electrons and protons.

Again, yin and yang can be thought of as complementary forces that interact to form a dynamic system in which the whole is greater than the assembled parts. The yin and yang bring about an amalgam of the two seemingly opposing forces. Everything in our universe has both yin and yang aspects; for instance, the shadow cannot exist without light, man does not exist without woman, etc.

In addition to being relative opposites that define one another, yin and yang are also dynamic, shifting, generating and evolving energies. In other words, there exists an intimate and active bond between them. On one hand, yin and yang seem to oppose one another creating conflict, tension, friction and discord. On the other hand, they complement one another creating active harmony, balance, equilibrium and stability. This paradox is the very nature of yin and yang. The ever going interplay of yin and yang result in the diversities of nature's shapes and forms, characteristics and phenomenological play; indeed, all of evolution itself is the result of this eternal balancing process.

The yin-yang symbol (*taijitu*) shows a balance between two opposites with a portion of the opposite element in each section. Yin (feminine) energy is depicted by the black section, while yang (masculine) energy is depicted by the white section. Notice that in the middle of the main black section of the yin, there is a white dot. And in the middle of the main white section of the yang, there is a black dot. Again, this connotes pictorially the concept of the interplay of seeming opposites.

In our teachings, the white section represents the masculine and within that part, the black dot represents the innate feminine within the male. The complementary of that principle is that the black section represents the feminine and within that part, the white dot represents the innate masculine within the female. This is important to understand in dream reading as we get further into the next section on anima and animus.

Some general characteristics of yin to remember are: feminine, feeling, passivity, yielding, nourishing, darkness, thickness, cold, decay, downward direction, inside. Some general characteristics of yang are: masculine, mind, thinking, doing, action, lightness, heat, protection, commanding, upward motion and outside.

A caterpillar dreamed she was a butterfly.
Upon awakening, she was confused.
Was she a caterpillar dreaming she was a butterfly?
Or a butterfly dreaming she was a caterpillar?
— Chuang Tzu

6. Anima and Animus

The soul of a woman is masculine. The soul of a man is feminine.
- Dr. Pat Allen

In dream reading, the importance of yin and yang leads us to Emma Jung's famous work on *anima* and *animus*, as well as to the important tenet of Pat Allen's work of Androgynous Semantic Realignment (ASR); that is, the ability to find a balance between the masculine and feminine aspects within oneself. Anima is the feminine Latin-derived word for a man's soul. Animus is the masculine Latin-derived word for a woman's soul. Anima and animus in Jung's school of psychology are the two primary anthropomorphic archetypes of the unconscious mind which we call yin and yang in our dream reading system.

Among other things, the anima (yin) is the unconscious drive of Eros in a man, finding expression as a feminine inner personality. In the unconscious of a woman, the animus (yang) represents the Logos, expressed as a masculine inner personality. However, both men and women express both anima (yin) and animus (yang) in dreams. The integration of anima and animus through dream work allows the individual greater freedom of behavior and outlook, as the accustomed restricted way of psychological functioning can be modified by a complementary viewpoint; that is, seeing the opposite gender energy within oneself.

This seeming paradox should be thought of as evidenced in the *taijitu* symbol, the swirling white and black in a circle, wherein there is a white dot in the black portion and a black dot in the white portion, indicating the complementary aspect of nature, including human nature, rather than the oppositional aspects we oftentimes perceive. The masculine white yang section contains the yin feminine black point; and conversely, the black yin feminine section contains the white yang masculine point. Yin and yang complement each other and the inversely complementary expression of yin feminine (anima) and yang masculine (animus) sides, especially as expressed in dreams, can seem counterintuitive.

To make this more comprehensible, we oftentimes see men suppressing their innate sensitivity, their yin feminine side, the anima. Therefore, the anima feminine, yin side that does exist in men gets expressed in dreams in order to alert a man to his healthy feminine feeling-centered side, relating to sensitivity, creativity, and instinct. A man over-expressing his feminine yin anima side is oftentimes wallowing in his reactive feelings, emoting in an unbalanced way and the dream can alert him to that issue.

Oftentimes a woman's innate animus masculine/yang side is expressed in her dream and can point to excessive mothering or over-achieving in the waking life. If there is a suppression of that yang side, it may express itself in a woman becoming overly-dependent or even a victim. Therefore, the animus masculine/yang side that does exist in women gets awakened in dreams in order for women to pay attention to and find balance with the healthy aspect of their masculine.

Remember that intuition is the ability to understand something immediately without the need for reasoning. Instead, we can understand that intuition is the extrapolation of intellectual data beyond conscious awareness. This process of awakening our other-gender sides is integral to our quest for healthy androgynous balance; that is, being able to access both hemispheres of the brain which are oftentimes related to general gender functions and may be skewed too much in one direction or the other.

Male figures appearing in dreams signify the feminine/yin feeling, physicality and the instinctive aspects which may as yet be unrecognized in the waking state. Remember, instinct is an innate physiological and temperamental behavioral response to external stimuli that is below consciousness, i.e. the feeling-centered aspect. Female figures appearing in dreams, represent the masculine/yang functions, and serve to rouse the latent male attributes of assertiveness, potency, thinking and wisdom, as well as creativity and intuition. However, it is important to remember that a male figure appearing in *either* a man or a woman's dream signifies feelings. And, a female figure appearing in *either* a woman or a man's dream, signifies the thinking or doing side of consciousness.

In the waking state, the unconscious anima female/yin side influences men's feelings in relation to people, nature and things. Likewise in the waking state, the unconscious animus masculine/yang side in women influences their thinking aspects in relation to people, nature and things. However, in dreams, the anima and the animus manifest in important symbolic ways. Again, paradoxically, male figures appearing in dreams represent the yin, feeling aspects of our unconscious that are striving to be expressed and acknowledged in one's life. And female figures appearing in dreams, represent the yang, unconscious thinking aspects that are striving to be expressed and acknowledged in one's life.

Dreams are the royal path to what Jung called the individuation process or the soul's journey. Each of us has a unique destiny to unfold, a unique path with unique gifts and talents to express in this lifetime. Recognizing the seemingly paradoxical, seemingly opposite but actually complementary aspects within each of us is the path to that wonderfully fulfilling individuation process. Through our investigation of dreams, and our understanding of these yin and yang aspects within ourself, and how they ultimately express themself in our waking state, these important principles become our most vital tools in the process of finding real happiness and balance in our life.

> *There will never be a man as strong as a woman is inside. And there will never be a woman as sensitive as a man is inside.*
> — Dr. Pat Allen

7. How to Capture Your Dreams

Capturing our dreams is the first step in learning how to read our dreams. You can remember your nightly dreams if you attach great importance to them, which is the motivating factor in recalling dreams, to get deeper into your true nature. Before retiring for the night, the ego should prepare to encounter its own deeper aspects. This should be done in a spirit of great interest and expectancy. First, leave an open dream journal with a pen or a recording device next to your bed. Now we set the limen. Remember, the limen state is the three to four minute period that you are in both between sleeping and waking, and waking and sleeping. You set the limen, preparing that fertile space where we can come to profound revelations, by articulating an issue or situation, or questioning an area where in your life you want clarity. That clarity is going to come from your unconscious, through your dreams. Let's break these concepts down.

Going to sleep normally is looked at as a simple period of extended rest. But for anyone who wants to experience the deeper mysteries of their own life, or simply to find answers to personal questions, sleep must be approached in a more reverent manner. Being in a drunken state, or medicated, or overeating will impair your ability to both dream and catch your dreams. There are more specific ideal conditions for dreaming and dream catching such as sleeping in a room where the temperature is comfortable (recommended is 60 to 68 degrees F. or 16 – 20 degrees C.). A quiet and dark place to sleep is also conducive to our purposes. Dark means that you eliminate all white, blue, and green lights that are emanating from devices such as your TV, DVR, computer, and mobile device at least two hours before sleeping and during

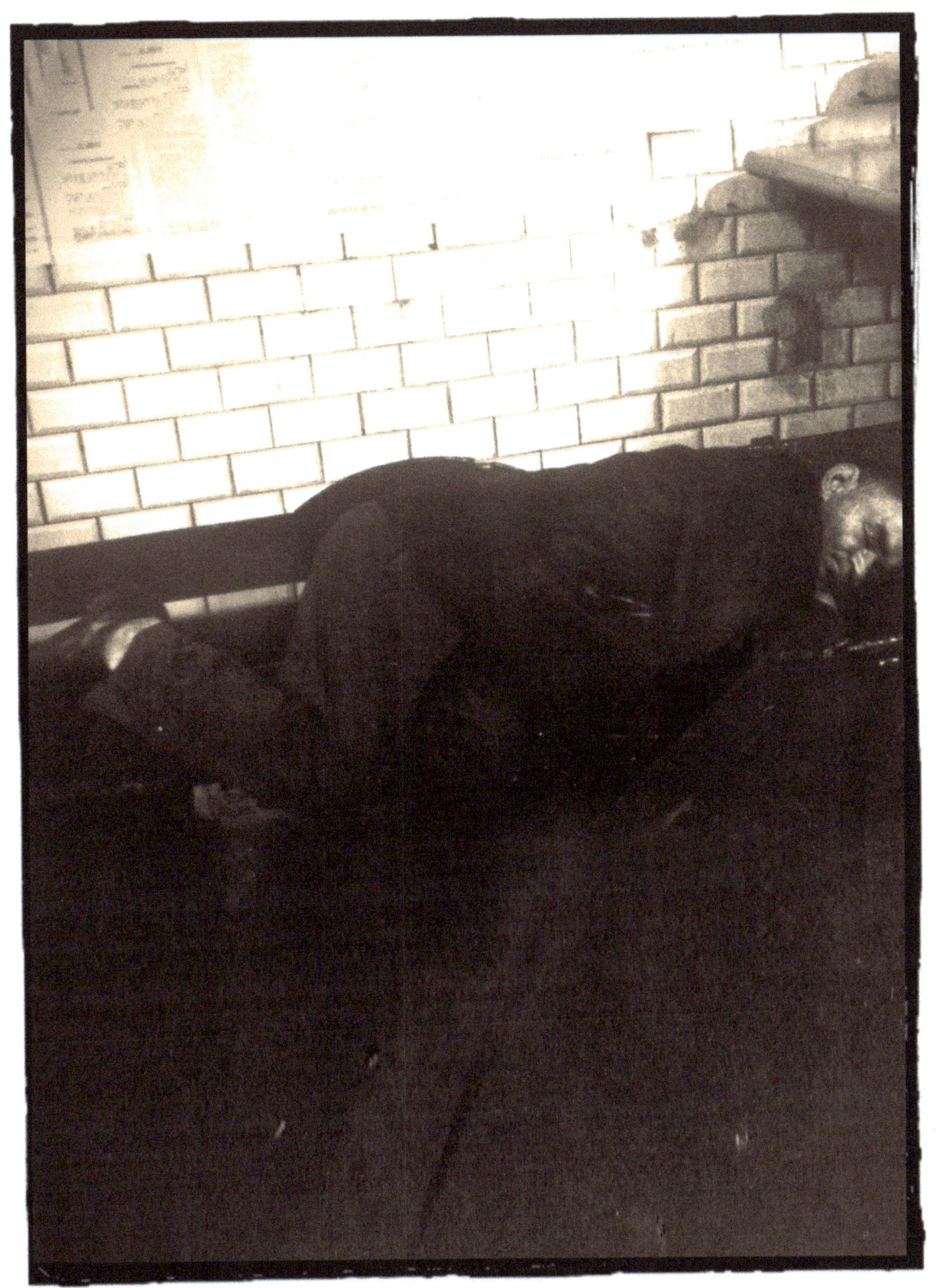

sleep. Except for amber and red light, all other light at night adversely affects the brain's melatonin level which is necessary for quality sleep.

You should have a special journal or diary reserved only for recording your dreams. Making your physical journal special helps you to focus your mind and purpose in this process. Don't write things to do with your next day schedule or some other non-dream related stuff in this special book. Of course, you can keep a separate daily journal to record what experiences you have had during the day. You can use your daily journal later side by side with your dream journal to see what corollaries exist between your dream life and your waking life.

Now we are prepared to set the limen by stating a specific issue, or by asking a question which will help the unconscious to get you in touch with your own instincts and intuition. You can choose to write a statement or question in your dream book for the purpose of getting deeper into this issue. Or, you can simply speak your statement or ask your question silently or aloud to yourself. Your statement or question should be made in broad terms. For example, sometimes you may have a financial issue that has not been resolved. In that case, you should *not* ask a question such as, "Where will the money come from to settle this matter?" Framing that issue as a statement or question in broader terms leaves an opening for the dream coming through your unconscious to give you more insights than your narrow question or statement.

For instance, in setting your limen you may state out loud or write in your dream journal, "I want insights into all the possibilities of how this financial situation can be resolved." You can also ask or state that you want this information not only for your own personal good but also for the good of others, or even for a greater non-personal purpose. In this way of opening the unlimited depths and power of your own unconscious, a dream may follow that reveals a bigger and better picture than you could have figured out in your conscious waking life.

When you start to wake up, stay in the limen state. This is very important for remembering your dream and the images in it. Keep your eyes closed for the 3 to 4 minutes that you are in the limen state. Understand that once you actually open your eyes, you are no longer in the limen state and the dream images and messages will fade and vanish. Remember, the limen is that threshold of consciousness between sleeping and waking. The dream is elusive and cannot wait for a time that is convenient for you to capture it. Don't think you can remember the dream later when you are fully awake. Write it down immediately! This is why many people say they do not remember their dreams. They have not mastered this simple but profound practice and discipline.

Do not move more than necessary before writing down your dream. That means don't go to the bathroom first or have a cup of coffee to wake up. It is important to keep still when you first awaken in the limen state as you may have only the tiniest image of the dream in your memory. That tiny image may only be an action or a thing, a place or a word, or even just a color. By keeping still with your eyes closed, you will remain partly in the dream state and you will be able to pull the dream back together by grabbing on to that image.

Once you have remembered even just this one piece of the dream in the limen state, you should write it down immediately, even scrawling that one piece of information down in your dream journal with your eyes still closed, or partially closed. Just scribble down anything that you remember. You can tie the pieces together later.

Oftentimes, just writing down this first image of the dream that you recollect will help you recall more pieces of the dream. Once you write down the first image, if you can stay in the limen state, perhaps another image may come up that you will also be able to write down. Write down every detail!

Another way to capture your dream in the limen state is to just stay still with your eyes closed for that 3 to 4 minute period and let images come up randomly before starting to write down your dream. By following any of these methods, you will be able to start tying more pieces together related to this dream.

The more you practice staying in your limen state while pulling one or more images of your dream together, the more adept you will become in fully capturing your valuable dreams. Again, writing the dream images down is done before any other normal waking-up activities. You are in essence making your dream more important than your immediate waking life.

Avoid adding extras in recording your dreams that you did not actually experience in the dream. That means do not start adding commentary on your dream, as putting in extra information will hinder the psychological understanding of the depicted dream symbols. "Just the facts, Ma'am," as one TV detective famously may put it. We get into meanings later. Again, take care to note the dream elements exactly as they appeared in the dream, without modifying anything. The ego always wants to protect itself by editing out whatever it does not find flattering to its persona ideals. So we have to be rigorously honest in recording material from the unconscious, exactly as it originally appeared, warts and all.

Encountering and capturing dreams in a slow, rhythmic, organic way is more reliable and profound than any quick or gimmicky means. The task is not to flood the waking state with material from the unconscious but rather to integrate these contents slowly into an open and receptive state of conscious wholeness. There is a lot in this process for the waking consciousness to ingest and digest, and the process is best accomplished a little at a time, slowly but surely.

> *What happens to our dreams?*
> *Whether we remember them or not,*
> *Where do they go?*
> *And from where do they come?*
> — Etan Boritzer, author
> *What is Dreaming?*

8. What is a Dream Reading?

Once you have your dream in hand, meaning that you saved it, you are ready to embark on your journey to find out what your dream is revealing to you. Whether you are going to revisit your dream with a *bona fide* dream analyst or try to read your own dream, it's important to understand what a dream reading is, and what it is not.

A dream reading is a tool (a barometer) for looking into our unconscious in an organized manner in order to help us become aware of any imbalances that we are encountering in every aspect of our waking life including financial hardships, business matters, relationship issues, and health and wellness concerns.

Dream reading is *not* fortune telling or a parlor trick. We are not trying to predict the future through our dreams, such as who will win the Kentucky Derby. However, our dreams point to where in the future (near or far) we need to direct our energies for well-being in our life. That means if we don't heed the message or warning in the dream, our unconscious patterns will repeat themselves and keep us from evolving. Conversely, if we do understand and decide to heed the message of the dream we may bring clarity to matters that are currently out of balance.

Dream reading is to be revered, as it has been historically in most cultures since ancient times. If you find you are getting some positive results through your dream readings, that there is a resonance between your dreams and your waking life, then continue to hone your skills rather than showing off your accomplishments. A dream reading is not to be used to manipulate or control other people. The dream reading is not about the dream reader. There cannot be any ego attachment to your abilities. These abilities are used solely to help yourself or others, whether or not you are being paid professionally for readings.

The dream reader must strive for ultimate objectivity in the reading. For example, if you are reading your husband's dream, you have to remember that you are there to help him, not you. If you help him come to clarity on some issues in his life through the dream reading, you should not slant your reading to your needs. This objectivity is a crucial discipline that needs to be developed and maintained because you can only truly help someone when you give them information that self-empowers them. That means that your objectivity allows the dreamer to make decisions and to take actions on their own, rather than through some subtle subjectivity you may be exerting on them. And whatever the dreamer's ultimate actions are, based on your dream reading, you cannot be attached to those actions, however well-intentioned or accurate your dream reading is for that person. In simple terms, you are merely holding up a mirror to that person. And remember, you are holding that mirror up with compassion. Thereafter, you have done your job.

These parameters are vital in starting your dream reading work. This is considered sacred work in most cultures and should be undertaken with seriousness. You are the medium connecting the unconscious to the conscious. In both ancient and many contemporary cultures, a person who does this work is called a shaman. Having a full understanding of what a dream reading is, and what a dream reading is not, is essential to your success. Set your intentions carefully.

9. How to Read Dreams

A dream not interpreted is like a letter not read.
- The Talmud

    We are oftentimes too close to our own predicaments to understand them at the deepest levels, in the same way that the nose on our face is too close for us to see without the help of a mirror. In reading dreams, the reader acts as the necessary mirror allowing for some perspective on our dreams. Therefore, at the beginning of our dream reading efforts, we may need some assistance in seeing the dream more clearly and more objectively. When someone works with the help of a dream reading expert who is empathetic, knowledgeable, astute and experienced it allows for a deeper personal interaction with our unconscious. Even when dreams are not interpreted, nevertheless their power has a marked effect upon our waking consciousness.

    In learning how to work through the complex process of dream reading, the main point is to understand the images that are bubbling up from the unconscious to the conscious mind. In that way, one can begin to ascertain the lessons that are being presented by the dream and how to better process one's personal journey through the waking life. Dreams can also be seen as guides on the deeper mystical journey of the soul. We must never think that our understanding of a particular dream has been complete. Subsequent dreams may throw more light on a situation and modify our understanding radically. Dreams are best studied in a series in order to grasp the full impact of the unconscious and its power.

The dream truly belongs to the dreamer in more ways than one. Ultimately the dreamer begins to resonate with the reading. Accurate interpretations will always ring true with the dreamer. It is important for the dream reader to ask questions after the dreamer has relayed the narrative and contents of their dream in order to get to the core of what the unconscious is revealing to us. An experienced dream reader will question the dreamer on a particular image and how the dreamer relates personally to that image. The dream reader can start with a question such as, "What character qualities does that person in your dream embody?" If the dream involves an animal such as a dog, the dream reader can ask, "How do you feel about dogs, do you like them or dislike them?"

Remember that every symbol in the dream is actually a part of the dreamer's own psyche in whatever aspect that part comes alive in the dream narrative. Personally, I usually don't explain this facet of dreaming early in the gathering-of-information part of the reading. This is an important contextual framework in our system of dream reading and I only discuss this aspect at a time when it will help the dreamer to reveal deeper truths about themself.

The dream reader interpreting a dream subjectively and giving only general dream symbol meanings will not truly serve the dreamer. Remember that the dream is looking at things with its own slant, from an angle sometimes far removed from that of the waking-ego. Again, we may not see the "forest for the trees." Training, skill and care in dream reading are truly needed by an individual attempting to work on their dreams alone, or to help others.

As a dream reader, you start by writing down some of the key images being relayed to you. In order to get specific and refined information about the dream you can start by asking a question such as, "What is the first image or part of the story you remember?" Many times the locale gives you lots of information on its own. For example, water in a dream almost always relates to the sensual/sexual side of ourself (feminine/yin). Being up in the mountains or on the upper floors of a building relate to being up in one's head (masculine/yang) and can relate to the business, work, action or the doing side of one's life. I will give you further information on the important aspects of yin/yang in the following chapters.

Start the dream reading from the first thing the dreamer remembers. For example, they may say something right away such as, "I was at a beautiful tropical beach." You can now start asking deeper questions such as, "How close were you to the water? Were you walking toward it or away from it? Was the water clear, calm and inviting or tempestuous?" These types of questions help us to hone in on how the dreamer thinks and feels about the relationship aspects of their life.

If the dreamer is up somewhere in the mountains which might metaphorically represent being up in one's head, the masculine thinking/yang side of life, ask questions such as, "Were there other people or animals around the locale? Was there snow, or just trees?" Again, the more details we gather about the location in the dream, the more help we get in understanding the dream.

Then, you can start going deeper into the symbols. The symbol of water, as mentioned, usually relates to the sensual and sexual side of our life. If it is mountains, or some elevated locale such as a tall building, this might metaphorically relate to the mental or the thinking/action side of life such as work. These are just some examples at this point of the approach to speculating on possible archetypal influences in the dream. Then you can begin to ask questions in the dream reading that relate to the dreamer's personal associations.

Sometimes knowing the location of the dream is not as immediately important as knowing the situational aspect of the dream. The dreamer may be dealing with a particular situation where the locale may not even be a prominent feature. For example, there may be a confrontational situation wherein a child dreams that he is being chased by a bear. He may just express that part of the dream initially because to him the location is less important than the immediacy of the situation.

In our teachings, we prioritize matters in a dream through the three main symbols: **People**, **Nature** and **Things**. There is a measured desensitization by the unconscious to our most sensitive issues as most of the time our unconscious is kind and does not want to shock us. We call this *gradual desensitization*, the process by which our unconscious prepares us for difficult issues that we are moving through in our waking life. Dreaming about things is an entry-level knock on your conscious door by the unconscious. Dreaming about various nature images takes us up the ladder in terms of clarity, bringing greater attention to an issue. When people appear in a dream it means we are coming the closest to an awareness of the connection between our dream/unconscious and conscious/waking life, moving to truer perceptions regarding the circumstances and situations around us.

Draw out as much information about the dream before you start to read it. Sometimes asking for more information triggers more memories of the dream and that allows for a more accurate reading of the dream. The dreamer may even remember a previous dream as they start to relay the particulars of one dream.

You can ask about associations that the dreamer may have to particular people, nature images or things in the dream. Symbols are really coded associations. For example, what does the symbol of a Doberman pinscher mean to the dreamer? That dog symbol will connote a different association from one dreamer to the next. There are also archetypal symbols that need to be individually looked at to further personalize the reading. Remember that part of the dream reader's job is to coax out the meaning of the symbols and circumstances and to help the dreamer to connect the dots as to how the dream relates to their waking life situations. Drawing out information from the dream requires patience, insight and a sixth sense so that the dreamer is inspired to move deeper into the issues that the unconscious is asking you to explore.

Once you have gleaned as much information about the dream as you can, start to go into the all-important energy aspects, the yin/yang of the dream. If a male figure appears in a dream it represents the feminine/yin within the dreamer, meaning the feeling-centered side of the dreamer. This is true whether the dreamer is male or female. If a female figure appears in a dream it represents the masculine/yang within the dreamer, meaning the doing, thinking side of the dreamer. This is also true whether the dreamer is male or female.

Dreaming of nature and things indicates a further necessity to understanding the yin and yang aspects. Generally speaking in nature, cats and other small, furry creatures, flowers, small birds, etc. are considered yin aspects. In nature, mountains, trees, various animals such as dogs and larger animals, and large predatory birds are considered yang aspects. While it is impossible here to catalog all of nature in terms of yin/yang, as one develops greater experience in dream reading, the particular yin/yang aspects in nature become more evident. In regards to things appearing in a dream, objects that are soft and comfortable, smooth or silky textured, even plush furniture are considered yin aspects. In regards to things appearing in a dream, objects that are hard, rough, mechanical, metallic, concrete are considered yang aspects. As the dream reader gains more skill, they also start to develop a greater feel in interpreting the yin/yang aspects of nature and things, thus leading to deeper insights for the dreamer.

As we have said, it is also important to understand the Jungian anima/animus paradox wherein men unconsciously express their feminine side for psycho-emotional balance. And conversely, women unconsciously express their masculine side for balance. This is the way to a healthy balance between our masculine and feminine sides. This paradox is sometimes a difficult concept to understand or accept but if you contemplate it further, you can see how it is true in both our dreaming states and our waking life.

Once yin aspects of the dreamer are awakened and identified, we can begin to know where those feelings and sensations can be addressed in the waking life and start to achieve more balance. When yang aspects of the dreamer are awakened and identified, we can begin to know where those thoughts, ideas and behaviors can be addressed in the waking life and start to achieve more balance.

Working with this seemingly paradoxical concept is essential to our unique teaching. And, the more you work with this yin/yang relationship within the dream context, the more accurate your readings will be for yourself and for others. The connections will soon open your eyes to how these paradoxical mysteries really work in our life. You start understanding where your own imbalances are within and how those imbalances affect you in your conscious waking life.

Archetypes, another Jungian concept, also help us in reading the dream. Archetypes are objective, large concepts that are globally recognized. While these archetypes can take on numerous forms in our dreams, there are several archetypal images that commonly occur in most cultures. It is important to note, however, that the context in which these archetypal images appear is just as important as the image itself as it may refer to a specific personal connotation and meaning. For example, the archetype of a child appearing in a dream might signify new and emerging thoughts or feelings. Going further into archetypal associations would depend on factors such as the gender or race of the child. And, those associations also depend on the dreamer's own cultural, racial or religious affiliations. The dream reader has to take the general archetypal image and help the dreamer to see the personal connotation. A crone or old woman appearing in a dream can be viewed as a cultural archetype of ancient wisdom or old ideas; whereas an old man appearing in a dream can represent old feelings or even a spirit guide coming through the unconscious. Again, the personal significance of the archetype needs to be uncovered.

If we continue to deny or suppress old emotional wounds, traumas, even everyday unexpressed thoughts and feelings, they grow stronger within and can sabotage our life through misdirected behaviors. The unconscious precedes the conscious, from the inside out. That means that if we do not investigate the unconscious, particularly through dreams, we will continue to repeat negative habitual patterns. By bringing attention to and eventually clearing out our hidden issues relating to fears, resentments, animosities or various guilts, we can begin to heal ourself from the inside out. When we create space within the unconscious through dream readings it makes room in our psyche to allow for new, more creative and healthy ways to live our life. Again, our goal in reading dreams is to free ourself from blockages or imbalances, or simply to get a psychological status update so that we may live our life optimally.

10. Common Dream Themes

If the mouth can't say it, the body will demonstrate it.
— Dr. Pat Allen

There are general dream themes that are helpful to discuss here. While these are broad areas that our unconscious is talking about to us, remember as we have said, that the interpretation of these thematic elements ultimately remains very individualistic. These motifs, therefore, should help lead the dreamer or dream reader to more specific and personal questions that will reverberate through to their waking life. Also, recall that in the below themes we often refer to the feeling/yin side and the thinking/yang side of the dream's concerns.

Death

Something has to die in order for something to be born. Death can be seen as necessary for a new beginning to occur. Are there people, ideas or feelings that no longer serve the dreamer, that the dreamer is ready to release? We use the expression *the creative void* to connote a personal or universal space. This idea may appear in the dream as a death but which is actually space created in the unconscious that can then be filled with new and better thoughts and feelings leading the dreamer ultimately to a more fulfilling life.

Drugs and Drinking

People drink and use drugs in order to knock out their thoughts or feelings. Is there something the dreamer wants to avoid? When women drink, they knock out their feelings and become more masculine. When men drink, they knock out their thinking and become more feminine. Alcohol and drugs are not the way to achieve a healthy balance in life but in this type of dream, the unconscious is telling the dreamer that there is something they don't want to deal with in their waking life. Note that for someone who is a recovering alcoholic or drug addict, this type of dream acts as a sort of pressure valve that allows a kind of release, or a *free party*, as we call it. However, this dream theme does not necessarily indicate a relapse.

Examinations

Examinations, tests and competitions in dreams may be metaphors for examining oneself, or one may feel they are being tested. How is the dreamer performing in their waking life? Are they being tested in their love life, or some other relationship, or professionally? What aspect of their life where they must prove themself is making them anxious?

Falling

Falling dreams usually indicates that the dreamer is moving from their thinking center down into their feelings. For a woman, an anxiety dream like this may occur when she is coming out of her thinking/work mode and into her physical/feeling mode. In a man's dream, however, he may be falling out of his mental potency or work goals into his feminine vulnerability. The expression *falling in love* is literally falling out of your thinking head into your physical/feelings. In order to understand the personal meaning for the dreamer, it is best to ask them what they were feeling as they were falling in the dream and how that might relate to feelings about a waking life situation they are in at the time.

Flying

In this type of dream, the dreamer is up in their head and handling life from thinking-centeredness instead of from the lower gut feelings. The unconscious may be indicating that one is not grounded, perhaps trying to escape feelings. Flying is a yang male experience, action and achievement-oriented. When a woman dreamer is flying, she is up in her head and not as much in touch with her feelings, perhaps too much in her business or male yang mode. Similarly, if a male is flying, it means that he is in his thinking-centeredness and moving away from his feelings. Flying up, meaning into the head area, may indicate a business or work project that the dreamer is engaged in, or about to be engaged in, working things out rationally or being in control. The dreamer may have freed themselves from a tough situation or has achieved a recent goal. Fear of falling during a flying dream represents a fear of going down into feelings. On the other hand, floating down may be experienced as a pleasant feeling.

Lost

When a dreamer is lost in their dream, i.e. wandering in some unknown locale or unable to get home can metaphorically picture a lack of direction in regards to a particular issue, or in the greater scheme of life goals. Lost at sea might indicate some drift or confusion in the sensual/sexual relationship side of life. Being lost in a high place such as in the mountains can represent some perplexity or uncertainty in the business or working aspect of the dreamer's life.

Money

Money can represent our precious life energy or a person's sense of self-worth. How is the dreamer protecting that energy? Is there some anxiety over losing personal life energy or losing potency in some area of the dreamer's life? There is emotional, physical, mental and spiritual currency in which we all deal on a daily basis. How is the bank where the dreamer keeps that currency? Is there enough in reserve, or available when needed? Is the dreamer feeling secure in their life or insecure?

Nudity

Dreams that involve nudity or even partially-clothed persons indicates that the unconscious is talking about an individual's persona, their outward, everyday self. It can mean that the authentic self is bare and exposed without the usual everyday armor or shielding. Nudity dreams indicate either a confidence in exposing one's vulnerabilities, or if there is embarrassment or hiding of the nakedness it means the dreamer is uncomfortable in allowing themselves to be vulnerable or exposed and should pay attention to areas in their life where they are uneasy. One may, or may not, be embarrassed by the nakedness or exposure of the real self. In a naked dream, one can also feel comfortable in their own skin and show their authentic self.

Pregnancy

What potential is being released in the dreamer's life or psyche? What new project is the dreamer embarking on, or what situation is embryonic and about to manifest? A pregnancy dream may indicate an anxiety or a celebration of what is about to emerge in the dreamer's waking life.

Sex

Is there a coercion into sexual situations? Sometimes there are sex dreams about being raped, molested or violated. Since the personage in the dream always represents the dreamer themself, one may be embracing a feeling or thinking part of themself. Sometimes a dreamer is just having a wet dream, a release of sexual tension or again, a *free party*. Dreams that depict androgyny in which the dreamer mutates from one gender to the other represent an integration of one's masculine and feminine sides. A sexual act in the dream or even just an embrace between male and female can also point to this integration of one's masculine and feminine.

A dreamer, male or female, making love to a woman shows that they are embracing their male productivity. A dreamer, male or female, making love to a man shows that they are accepting of their feelings. These are the paradoxical notions of a female figure appearing in the dream representing the yang/doing side, and that of a male figure in the dream representing the yin/feeling side. There are no homosexual or lesbian connotations related to the gender of the dreamer's sex partner. Remember that each figure or symbol in the dream represents an aspect of the dreamer's own self and should not be read literally. Sometimes the dreamer may simply be having a "wet dream" or as I have referred previously to the notion of a *free party*.

War

How stressful is the dreamer's working and/or home life? Are they stressed to the point of blowing up? Who or what is the dreamer wanting to fight? Or is the dreamer being attacked and from what area in their life? Dreaming of war may represent an inner conflict that is in need of a resolution. Or it may indicate a battle of wills, opposing viewpoints or an argument with someone. The unconscious may be pointing to some area of chaos and disorder in the waking life. War may also symbolize some aggressive behaviors that one is not conscious of or bring an awareness of an abusive relationship that is occurring in the dreamer's life.

II. Dream Symbols

The symbol is neither abstract nor concrete, neither rational nor irrational, neither real nor unreal.

- Carl Jung

Symbols are the keys to unlocking the mysteries of the unconscious, helping us to navigate the unknown. In our conscious waking life, the visual images that our eyes catch are taken literally. A homeless woman is a homeless woman, a car is a car, a lake is a lake, etc. In dreams, the images we see are *not* literal—they are symbols or representations of a figurative nature. In our dream life, the mind provides nuances, shadings and subtler realities that we are unaware of in our waking life. Because many of our most profound experiences in life are inexplicable, dreams provide symbols as a special pictorial and metaphorical language to give us a clearer understanding of things we may not understand or want to understand, in our daily life.

When symbols manifest in dreams, they resonate meaningfully to us but in their own non-rational way because it is difficult to describe or translate our deepest self and our deepest concerns into simple, ordinary words. The visual images we see in our dreams, appearing in symbolic forms, can be truly awe-inspiring and full of revelatory information that we could not otherwise perceive in our waking life.

Dream symbols are never consciously devised. They emanate from both the personal unconscious and the realm of the collective unconscious. By their very nature, dreams and the symbols they conjure up relieve the tension of opposites within the psyche by opening up new paths of perception thereby unblocking the flow of physic energy. The symbols in our dreams help point the way out of conflict and confusion, or they may simply confirm some deep truths that we have not recognized which may validate certain safe paths we have already undertaken.

Our innermost Self often cannot be fully defined with words. Symbols carry the ego-mind beyond its definitive and limited everyday dimensions. Symbols in this sense are non-rational carriers of meaning from the hidden realm of the unconscious to the ordinary everyday realm of consciousness.

The Self that we are, and how it is revealed in symbolic forms in dreams is a fascinating and complex entity, more profound than we realize in our waking life. Understanding the Self through the language of symbols provides a sense of universal and personal sacredness. Symbols are pregnant with meaning but they are not simple explanatory signs. The dream images provide hints as to the contents of the unconscious, pointing to energies and realities which transcend conscious categorization.

All of us have some secret innate fears lurking in our unconscious. We may have fears of the inexplicable and chaotic nature of human life on this planet. We also have wonderful holistic qualities which seek to be expressed from the unconscious to the conscious. The wish to make all aspects of our life understandable is a basic drive. To have an appreciation of these inherent, non-rational impulses describes the very nature of symbols. When symbols manifest in dreams, if we allow them to resonate meaningfully in their non-rational way, we can discover either a simple answer to a personal conundrum or even gain profound insights into our deeper Self.

People, Nature and Things

The three major categories of dream symbols are represented by people, nature and things. When we dream at the level of things it means that the message of the dream is just starting to bubble up from our unconscious. At the level of nature dreams, we are getting closer to what the dream is trying to teach us. When we are at the level of dreaming of people, we are closest to understanding the lesson of the dream as it relates to us in a most personal way. Why is our unconscious providing these three basic levels of symbols? The answer, simply put, is that the unconscious astutely prepares us to learn the dream information at the level that we are ready to receive that information emotionally, intellectually, or even spiritually.

People

Dreaming of people is the way in which the unconscious brings the dreamer the most immediate, precise and pertinent personal information, more so than dreaming of nature or things. Dreaming of people is the closest the unconscious comes to the conscious, meaning that a person appearing in the dream represents a personality characteristic of the dreamer themselves. Remember that every symbol or image in the dream is really an aspect of the dreamer.

Dreaming of people as symbols includes all types of males and females of all ages, in all categories comprised of infants, children, teenagers, young adults, adults, old people, family and relatives, business or work associates, neighbors, strangers, people with distinctive characteristics, historical, religious notables, political figures, celebrities, artists, scary people, goblins, fairies, ghosts, and mythological figures. The individual attributes of the people appearing in our dreams is important to understand. For example, was the witch you dreamed of old or young,

what was her ethnicity, her attire or demeanor? Again, all of the attributes of the people we dream of are attributes of our personality and our current conditions or circumstances. The witch then can represent your own old scary thoughts or ideas.

Nature

Nature as symbols represented in dreams relates to our natural origins and instincts, and signifies the second level of our gradually opening awareness. This means we are getting more ready to accept the lesson that our dream is bringing to us. Nature symbols come to us as animals; some of the most common ones are horses, dogs, cats, birds, fish, insects and reptiles, etc. Environmental elements may also appear in the dream; such as water, trees, rocks, mountains, beaches, deserts, weather, sunlight and moonlight.

Remember that each of the symbols on the nature level can be very diverse. For example, the water element can be dreamt of as an ocean, a puddle, a shower, a swimming pool, lake, stream, or waterfall, even something as simple as a leaking faucet. Water is a general and very common nature dream symbol for relationships and the sensual/sexual aspects of the dreamer's current or historical situation in those areas of their life. A nature dream involving water gives us a general direction to the message from the unconscious. If one dreams of a tree, for example without leaves, that can indicate a person's lack of self-esteem as a tree without leaves is not flourishing or maybe is in a winter or dormancy state.

Things

When things such as inanimate objects appear as a dream symbol it means that something you should pay attention to in your life is just barely starting to come up into your consciousness. We dream of things because there is a trepidation within us that limits our personal development at a particular stage from going to the deeper places we must visit in order to truly *Know Thyself*. So, dreaming of things gradually gets us used to accepting messages coming from the unconscious.

Some common things that arise as symbols in our dreams are vehicles such as cars, buses, even airplanes, boats and trains. Buildings can come in forms of skyscrapers, cottages, tool sheds, tents, fire stations, apartment buildings, and hospitals. You may dream of a room such as a doctor's office, classroom, bedroom, an empty room, a closet, kitchen or garage. Other things we can dream of are pictures, money, art, furniture, jewelry, clothes, tools, computers, phones, appliances, food, drink, or drugs.

In order to understand the personal associations with these things, we ask the dreamer what the purpose or function is of that thing. For example, in a dream that contains a door, we would determine the general purpose of a door. Then we ask the dreamer, what are you passing through in your life? Is the door open or closed? This dialogue helps the dreamer to relate to something in their life they are passing through such as a phase in their life, or if there is a blockage, or easy entry or exit in some circumstance or situation.

12. Common Dream Symbols

While there are dictionary-style dream books that list thousands of dream symbols and their meanings, our list below is meant only to be a preliminary introduction to some of the most common symbols that people find in their dreams. However, it's important to keep in mind that each symbol, general or specific, can have many different meanings depending on the type of that particular symbol and the dreamer's personal associations to that symbol. For example, a dream in which a dog appears points to a general archetypal symbol that can embody many meanings. While the common symbol of a dog is foremost a yang or masculine symbol, the dog symbol can be read differently as an archetype of fidelity and companionship, guardianship or aggressiveness. Bill and John both dreaming of a dog, even the same breed, may have different associations and receive different messages from their individual unconscious.

It is essential to ask more specifically, what size, breed or type, or color, etc. is the dog in your dream? If you dream of a Doberman pincher or toy poodle, there is a different reading considering the different characteristics and associations related to that dog symbol. The dog in your dream may be read differently if you love dogs or if you fear dogs. Again, one of the difficulties in dream reading is to remember that the reading of a symbol in one dream can be different than the reading of another individual's dream of the same symbol, depending on the specificity of the symbol and the dreamer's personal associations with that symbol. Below are some of the common symbols that we will often see in our dreams and in reading dreams.

Age

Past, present and future. The age of a symbol (people, nature or thing) gives us an indication of either the developmental stage of a feeling or a thought in the dreamer's unconscious. If there is an old man (yin image) in the dream, for example, that means one is becoming aware of an old feeling. Whereas, an old woman (yang image) appearing in the dream references an old idea arising from the unconscious.

Articles

Articles include all kinds of furniture or personal belongings such as wallets, purses, jewelry, valuables, as well as tools such as an ax, shovel, hammer, or kitchen utensils like knives and forks. Articles are categorized as either yin (feminine receptive/feeling aspects) or yang (masculine/doing aspects). Some articles are considered androgynous, meaning containing both yin and yang qualities. Dreams wherein articles appear as prominent symbols should be analyzed for the personal relationship to the article, i.e. losing your wallet (yang) will relate to the fear of one losing one's ideas of personal identity and security. The simplest way to determine the dreamer's own association with an article is to ask and help the dreamer to define the function or purpose of the article.

Body Parts & Health

This includes limbs, sensory parts such as ears, eyes, tongue, genitalia, buttocks, breasts, bodily fluids, bodily health symbols including injuries, ailments and conditions. When a body part figures noticeably in a dream the unconscious is pointing the dreamer toward something that may need attention energetically. For example, if there is an ear injury in the dream it might be a metaphor for something the dreamer does not want to hear or is not listening to in their life. We see the ear as a yin symbol (feminine/feelings)

as women are more auditory-oriented than men. If there is an eye image in the dream, we note that as a yang symbol (masculine/mental) as men are more visually oriented.

Buildings

Homes, mansions, castles, farmhouses, haunted houses, churches or temples, apartments, outhouses. Larger buildings such as skyscrapers and office buildings, hospitals, apartment complexes, jails, fire stations, airports, train stations, warehouses, restaurants, supermarkets and shopping malls. Dreaming of any building symbol relates generally to the dreamer's current situation in their life representing the embodiment of the dreamer's whole self or identity, their general state of being at the particular time of the dream.

For example, dreaming of a bank can indicate various personal life motifs such as security, hoarding, scarcity, wealth, etc. Where the dreamer actually finds themself in the building is important. Dreaming that one is in a basement shows that the dreamer is in their gut or feeling/yin center. Dreaming of being in an attic or in the upper stories of a building indicates that one is in their head or thinking/yang center. Seeing oneself outside of the house represents the dreamer viewing their life from an outside position, signifying they are detached or disconnected from themself. A church dream can reflect the spiritual self or more specifically, the associations the dreamer has with a church. If the dreamer is in a house with no doors or windows, they can't get in or get out, it could mean that they are stuck somewhere within themself. Buildings in general represent the dreamer's relationship with the Self.

Clothing

Outer clothing, underwear, seasonal clothing such as winter wear or bathing suits. Uniforms such as sports uniforms, military, police, fireman, nurse, pilot, sea captain uniforms, body armor, historical costumes, business suits, also lack of clothing or nudity. Clothing can be thematically understood as the dreamer's persona or the identity they present to the outside world. Underwear in a dream, depicted in any condition from torn to elegant, is a foundational layer of the dreamer's identity. Dreams of outerwear such as coats are ways that the unconscious depicts how the dreamer is protecting or armoring themselves, not allowing vulnerability nor revealing their authentic self.

Colors

Natural or unnatural colors. Black and white images. Qualities of colors such as intensity, iridescence, glowing, vivid or muted colors. Typically, we don't notice colors in our dreams but a particular color or color quality of the dream that stands out will add extra emphasis and meaning for that symbol. Research into colors in dreams has found that dream colors, as they do in waking life, relate to our subliminal human emotional responses. Each color excites a slightly different range of responses in the autonomic nervous system and the brain. For example, red excites the nervous system into making us ready for action but it can also stimulate passion. Blue calms the system, making us inclined to rest or turn our focus within. The interpretation of a particular color, or a specific emotion associated with it, may be different in the reading for two individuals depending on their personal history or cultural background. Chakras or mystical colors will be further discussed in the book and these have a more archetypal correlation than do ordinary colors.

Games

Sports games such as football, basketball, etc. video games, cards, board games. Games in dreams may indicate a scheming or strategizing time in the dreamer's life with qualities of competitiveness and drive, one-upmanship in business matters or advancement. The dreamer may be getting geared up for a challenge in their life. Of course, the other players in the game or competition have to be factored into the dream interpretation, as well as locale and other symbols present in the dream.

Food & Drink

All sorts of foods from every food group apples to zucchini, meat, fish, sandwiches, gourmet meals, sweets, cakes and deserts, plus drinks such as alcohol, coffee, tea, water. Food dreams can represent how one is symbolically being nourished or not being nourished in their life. Being deprived of love one may dream of food and drink as a form of self-pleasuring. The meaning of a feast or banquet in a dream can be a symbol of abundance, of achieving a degree of material security and even success that can now be celebrated after a period of struggle, financial hardship or difficulty.

Furniture

Tables, chairs, sofas, closets, refrigerators, stoves, mirrors, pictures and sculptures. As said before, buildings represent our current psychological state or situation in life. Therefore, if there is some prominent furniture symbol that appears in the dream the unconscious is pointing to a more specific aspect within the dreamer's current state. Of course, there is a multitude of furniture symbol interpretations but just for example, a few references can be made here. A minimal amount of furniture or plain furniture can represent low self-esteem. Whereas comfortable or elegant furniture connotes a state of well-being. Broken furniture may indicate that the dreamer is not feeling supported. Old furniture brings up the past reflecting that one's unconscious is becoming ready to deal with painful, nostalgic or even fun experiences from an earlier period in one's life.

Locales

Cities, ranches, gardens, historical places, mountains, beaches, trails, streets, neighborhoods, jungles. The locale that the dreamer finds themself in is oftentimes important as the locale represents how the dreamer is perceiving their world. Dreaming that one is in the mountains signifies that one is more in the yang/masculine thinking side of the psyche; that is, perceiving life more from their head rather than from their yin/feminine feeling side. If the locale is a beach that would indicate that the unconscious is referencing the sensual/sexual relationship side of the dreamer's life due to the proximity of water. Again, keeping in mind the need for an individual reading of each dream, a rustic setting for a dreamer who grew up in the country can reference one's roots or comfort zone but for an individual who grew up in the city, the rustic setting can represent a sense of freedom or relief from some pressures in the waking life.

Mythological

Dragons, fairies, monsters, ghosts and ghouls, witches, mythological figures such as centaurs, mermaids and science fiction characters. When there is a dream of a mythological figure we should refer in general to archetypal meanings, then go to the personal, individual meaning for the dreamer. These non-human figures arising from the deep unconscious indicate that one is not yet fully in touch with one's evolving psychological state but moving closer to a more real personal consciousness. As referenced previously, our unconscious knows what messages we are prepared to receive.

Therefore, our dream symbols arise in the hierarchy of people, nature and things. Mythological figures fall between the categories of people and nature. For instance, the mythological mermaid is more aligned with nature than with humans. The mermaid is not a fully human figure who lives underwater representing universal sexuality and has no feet to ground it. The dream reader might ask the person who has dreamed of a mermaid, "What is it that you are not doing functionally in your sexual/sensual relationship that makes you not grounded in yourself and possibly overly-concerned and giving too much to those around you."

People

Family, spouses, parents, elderly, children, friends, business associates, strangers, people in uniforms, various professionals. When one is dreaming of people, the dreamer is moving closest to consciousness of a particular area that the unconscious is addressing. The basic premise in our system of dream reading is that any person appearing in one's dream represents an aspect of the dreamer themself. A male appearing in the dream is reflecting the feminine/yin aspect of the dreamer's psyche, whereas a female appearing in the dream is reflecting the male/yang aspect of the dreamer's psyche.

We ask the dreamer what character qualities the person in the dream possesses in order to determine what kinds of feelings or thoughts are emerging for the dreamer. If a parent appears in the dream the unconscious is telling the dreamer about a family script issue; that is, a pattern of habitual behaviors that were inculcated into the psyche by the age of three. A figure appearing in a uniform relates to issues with authoritarian matters. The dreamer may be experiencing forms of forced outside control or one's own judgments or in a more positive light, the dreamer may be feeling their own confidence or their own powers of authority.

Teeth

Teeth generally relate to potency. Teeth-related dreams can represent a sinking into something, as in the phrase "to sink your teeth into it." The dreamer is ready to bite into life with conviction, to take action expressing with assurance and confidence. A dream wherein one breaks or loses teeth is associated with feelings of powerlessness and loss of control, i.e. losing potency in some area of the dreamer's life, anxieties over decisions, unpreparedness, or embarrassment.

Trees

Trees can represent virility as well as feminine psychic energy and even internal security. Trees convey a slow and purposeful personal growth. As always, the type of tree in the dream will reflect the personal unconscious of the individual. For a female dreamer, the tree represents potency, such as her ability to say no to what she doesn't want. A tree with no leaves in a woman's dream represents a lack of ability to say no in order to protect herself. In a male's dream, a big tree points to his ability to say and go after what he wants in life. A forest dream metaphorically indicates a flourishing situation.

Underwater Creatures

Dreams of underwater creatures, even sea monsters can be seen as powerful unresolved issues looming deep in the dreamer's unconscious. These creatures, including fish, live underwater without air analogous to the amniotic fluid, the primal pre-birth environment from which we all emerged. What is there deep in the dreamer's psyche that is starting to emerge and is ripe to be addressed? These underwater creatures are sometimes threatening as they may lead us back to some primal experiences that have not been faced, even back to the womb.

Vehicles

Rafts, cars (all types), boats, trains, airplanes, bicycles, wagons. A vehicle in a dream can be an automobile, boat, or any mode of transportation, even shoes. The vehicle represents your way through life such as a luxury car or one that constantly breaks down. Here again, it is important to read deeper from the general theme into the personal so that we begin to understand what is the status of the dreamer's direction. For example, losing one's car or one's car breaking down connotes a lack of control over how one is progressing through their life. Shoes, as a more elemental form of transportation, are sometimes dreamt of as being lost which suggests the dreamer is gaining contact with the earth or their individual reality, pleasant or unpleasant.

Water

Oceans, lakes, rivers, ponds, swimming pools, waterfalls, puddles, geysers, frozen bodies of water, water dripping, rain, harbors, boiling water, ice cubes. Water or liquids represent the sensual/sexual or relationship aspects that our unconscious wants to bring to our awareness. Is the dreamer being swamped by a relationship? Struggling in water refers to one's feelings of vulnerability in a relationship. Is the dreamer about to give up on something that is overwhelming them especially in their romantic life? Even falling in love can be scary which is sometimes represented by drowning. Sometimes the dreamer is blissfully floating in a beautiful tropical body of water indicating that they are in harmony with their relationship side of life.

13. Colors

Colors compromise an entire set of important symbols that require a more detailed analysis. Knowing the color of your dream symbol is important because it describes the intensity of the symbol, as a sort of barometer of our thoughts or feelings. The color of the symbol relates to the entire subject of the dream. For example, if you dream that you are driving a red sports car, first we say that a car is generally a symbol of the way you are going through your life at this time. A red sports car can be a more intense symbol of a fun and zippy way you are operating currently in your life. But is the red sports car you are driving going uphill, downhill, on a windy road, or on a straightaway? Colors can be seen as trigger points to entering more deeply into our emotional energy centers, also known as *chakras*, for the purpose of balancing our life. More on chakras follows.

Colors can be very subjective and personal. The color of the symbol adds deeper dimensions to what is really going on in the dream and in our waking life. The color of the symbol and the subject matter also suggest moods and tones. Therefore, first consider the dreamer's personal associations with the color of the symbol in their dream. Does the color remind them of a particular person, a body part, a childhood toy, some other object or even a state of mind? For example, the color yellow may remind one of their childhood school bus but for someone else, it may remind them of the old yellow house where their grandmother lived.

However, what if there are no personal associations to the color of the symbol? Lack of clarity in recognizing dream symbol colors, muddiness, or even not

remembering colors can let us know that there is some fogginess, ambivalence or shadowy aspects related to the dream subject matter. If an object in the dream has a strange hue or an unusual color it may indicate an uneasy feeling or an aberrant condition. The more specific interpretation of that object depends on if it has yin or yang qualities. In general, these strangely-colored objects indicate that things may not be normal in our life, or even that something new, special or fantastical is opening up for us. These unusual colors in the dream can point to an unknown and more creative place that one is moving into in their life.

Very bright or intense colors are calling our immediate attention to something in our life that we should bring into greater focus. When these sorts of non-associative or unusual colors appear in our dreams, it's important to go back to the more archetypal or classic readings of colors, or chakras. The chakras are an access point and a tool that opens us up to the entire collective unconscious where answers lie that are beyond our conscious, everyday awareness.

Dreaming is the freedom to perceive worlds beyond the imagination.
- Carlos Castaneda

Chakras as Color Symbols

The word *chakra* derives from Sanskrit, the ancient language of India, and means *wheel*. Chakras are believed to be energy centers of the body in the esoteric traditions of Indian philosophy. There are seven major chakras that are thought to be part of our subtle energy body, located at specific points in our physical body. The subtle body can also be thought of as our non-physical body in the dream state. The chakras are connected by 70,000 energy channels. In yoga, the energy channels are called *nadis*, whereas in acupuncture they are termed meridians. There is believed to be connections between our physiological and psychic centers; or as we may say today, our body/mind connections. This theory posits that human life simultaneously exists in two parallel dimensions; one, the physical body and the other as the mental or non-physical body. Chakra theory points to how the body and the mind mutually affect each other. Below we describe the chakras, their associated colors and how these colors correlate to the symbols in a dream.

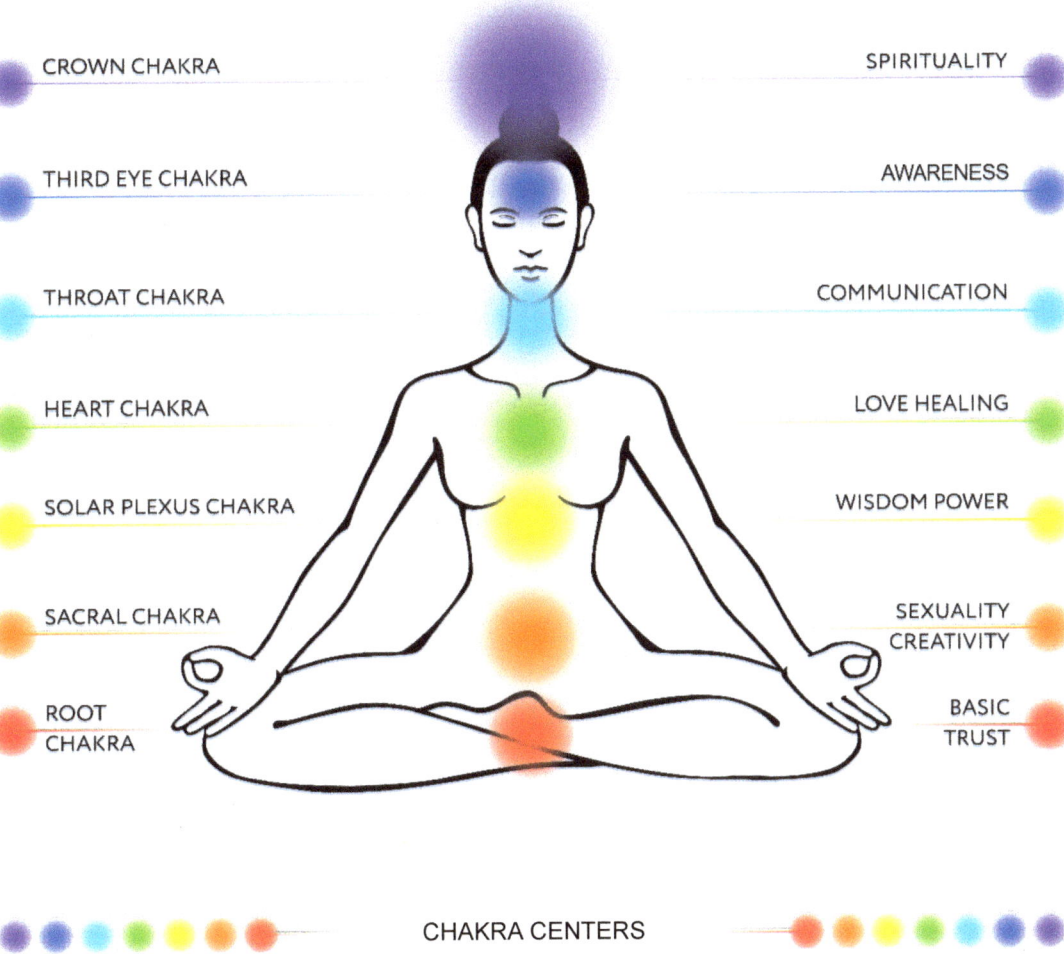

CHAKRA CENTERS

Red

    The Root Chakra (*Muladhara*; literally, *root support*) is a dense red color, representing the earth element. It is located physically at the perineum/coccyx area, near the base of the spine. The root chakra is a symbol of our survival, vitality and also our passions. The survival issues connected to this color may include things like money, financial independence and basic things like food. Therefore, it represents our human foundations and the crucial need in life to be grounded. The root chakra is also associated with courage, power, strength, love, war and desire.

    When one is in danger, this red root chakra arouses the fight or flight response. Additionally, the sense of smell is connected with this chakra energy center. Dreams that contain symbols depicted in red colors oftentimes signify danger, attracting our attention to that specific symbol because of its innate intense color. Red colors in a dream indicate our basic requirements for logic, physical strength, and orderliness.

orange

The second chakra (*Swadhisthana*; literally, *one's dwelling*) is orange in color, represents the water element and located at the reproductive glands, or the sacrum area. This chakra is a center of pleasure, sensuality, intimacy, and connection, as well as sexuality, creativity, desire, and passion. There is also a connection here to the sense of taste.

In dreams, symbols that come in orange colors can be associated with enthusiasm, happiness, attraction and joy. The main challenge that an orange symbol in the dream presents can be related to our conditioning by society where those types of feelings are not valued; where passion and emotional reactions are frowned upon or discouraged. Society often teaches us to disconnect from our bodies and our feelings of sexuality, enjoyment, and sensuality. However, remember that our dreams are not judgmental. Our second chakra dreams can show us that these areas are opening up for us. A person with an open second chakra is passionate, present in their body; sensual, creative, and connected to their feelings.

Yellow

Our third chakra (*Manipura*; literally, *jewel city*) is yellow in color, associated with the element of fire and is located in the solar plexus/navel region of the body. This chakra is the primary source of personal power associated with an individual's real life and professional success. Just as the sun charges our bodies and our moods with high volumes of energy, the activity of the solar plexus chakra gives us a sense of confidence, helping us to feel cheerful, energetic and encouraged. Producing the stimulating effects of warming and joy, dreams wherein symbols such as sunflowers appear can indicate an upbeat and energetic state of mind in one's waking state wherein intellect, energy, happiness, harmony, or wisdom are manifesting. On the other hand, if the dream symbol is depicted in an unpleasant yellow hue, then the dream can represent a state wherein fear, deceit, disgrace, betrayal, cowardice or sickness is being brought up to the dreamer's attention.

Green

The Heart Chakra (*Anahata*; literally, *unstuck*) relates to the element of air, is associated with green colors, and the sense of touch. This chakra is energetically responsible for all types of wholeness, relationships including love and marriage, compassion and bonding, involving the integrative, unifying and interconnected aspects of life. If one is dreaming of symbols in green hues and tones such as a lush green tree, it can mean that your life and relationships are flourishing. A dream symbol such as a dirty green car can mean that there is some distrust, envy or unfaithfulness, even illness being exhibited in the way that you are operating in your life. Indeed, most spiritual traditions recognize love as symbolized by the heart chakra as the ultimate healing force.

Blue

The fifth chakra (*Vishuddhi*; literally, *especially pure*) resides in the throat area, and is associated with the ethereal elements. The throat chakra is blue and is connected with a person's ability to communicate authentically and efficiently. The gift of this chakra is accepting your originality, expressing your genuine voice and speaking your truth. Ultimately, the activation and balance of the throat chakra inspires creativity, seeking and sharing of truths, and being open and honest. If one is dreaming of symbols in blue hues and tones such as a blue sail on a boat, you might want to pay attention to an area of communication in your relationships. Are you needing to vocalize something to your significant other so that you can work towards better communication with that person?

Indigo

The Third Eye Chakra (*Ajna*; literally, *inexhaustible*) transcends time. It is located in the brain at the pineal gland, at the mid-brow and is associated with the color indigo. This chakra enables people to see in a more discerning manner, activating the gift of truly seeing things as they are, not as they appear. When this chakra is activated there is a penetrating vision. We can see the outer world and attain deeper inner meanings. The energy of this chakra allows us to experience clear thought, as well as actuating spiritual contemplation and self-reflection. The energy of *Ajna* allows us to cut through illusion and to access deeper truths—to see beyond the mind, beyond words. If you dream of an indigo-colored object it can mean that you are having an accurate or clear vision about that symbol and the area it represents in your waking life. For example, if you are wearing an indigo jean jacket in a dream, it indicates you have a clear view of your persona as depicted by the outerwear symbol of the jacket as well as its indigo color.

Violet

    The seventh chakra is the Crown Chakra (*Sahasrara*; literally, *thousand petals*) and this chakra is violet in color. It is located at the crown of the head. The gift of this chakra is experiencing unity and a realization that everything is connected at a universal level, indicating a feeling of oneness with everyone and everything in nature. When the seventh chakra is activated one has a sense of knowing that there is a deeper meaning to life, that there is an order that underlies all of existence, an interconnectedness. If you dream that you are wearing violet-colored glasses, it can indicate that you are being drawn to look deeper at some spiritual area of your life. If you dream that you see a cracked violet window this could signal that there are some serious spiritual questions in your life that may need to be addressed.

Black

In physics, black is technically not a color because it has no wavelength; a black object absorbs all the colors of the visible spectrum, does not reflect itself back and is also considered the absence of light. Also, as any artist knows, if you mix all the colors of the color palette together, you will get black. Therefore, black is also the combination of all colors. In dreams, a black image typically symbolizes the unknown, the unconscious, danger, mystery, darkness, death, mourning, rejection, hate or malice. Black is a mysterious color that is often associated with something negative. However, it is also the color of yin actualization energies such as seriousness, power; even something formal, elegant, or prestigious.

Note that in various cultures the color black has different archetypal meanings. Considering these meanings can be helpful in reading our dreams from a general sense to the individual dreamer's needs. In Indian mythology, Kali is the black-skinned goddess and consort of Shiva the destroyer. *Kala* is the Sanskrit not only for the word black but also for time, meaning that Kali the goddess absorbs time and returns us to the unmanifested energies of the Universe, e.g. before the Big Bang. Note also that the archetypal Black Madonna and the Egyptian Goddess *Isis* also are black-skinned. The Black Madonna is celebrated by mystics who see this divine form of the Virgin as forever unknowable, mysterious, beyond all our concepts, hidden from all our senses in a light so dazzling it registers on them as darkness. The dark-skinned Isis represents life and rebirth with her outstretched wings representing her receiving and protecting the dead.

Black is the yin/feminine color with all the symbolic associations we have discussed previously. Jennifer dreamt of a black bra hanging on the door when her mother was ill and dying. The color black here represents her unconscious preparing for her mother's death. A bra is the first layer of clothing closest to a woman's heart. Further, as clothing represents persona, Jennifer's dream presages donning her other funeral attire. While the color black has universal associations, in dream reading again we have to recognize the individual's personal associations.

White

White resonates, like a silence that can suddenly be understood.
— Wassily Kandinsky

White is the combination of all the colors in the light spectrum and the indicator of light and brightness with powerful meanings linked to all human rites of passage. On the screen of a color television or a computer, for example, white is produced by mixing the primary wavelengths of red, green and blue at full intensity and giving off the color of light which is white. However, an artist may see white as a virgin canvas. Various cultures wear white for important occasions such as baptism, or white shrouds for funerals or white dresses for weddings. For many across the world, white symbolizes purity, innocence, holiness, mindfulness and perfection which are considered yang qualities. The color white can also symbolize the *tabula rasa*, an Aristotelian concept of the mind initially being like a blank slate on which eventually is written all our experiences, thoughts and emotions. In Asian cultures such as India and Japan mourners at funerals wear white, so there is a cultural subjectivity in dream color symbols and their interpretation, as we have discussed previously. White is also associated with cleanliness, spirituality, bliss, innocence, beauty and new beginnings. The white dove is now a standard symbol of peace. The white flag is a symbol of surrender. White is the color of masculine yang energy with all those symbolic associations that we have discussed previously. Frank dreamed of a woman in a long white dress walking toward an altar in a church. There were also other ladies in the church all wearing similar long white dresses facing the altar. I know from my sessions with Frank that at this time in his life he was considering leaving a business partnership which he thought lacked integrity. In the dream, Frank is moving toward spiritual integrity in thought and action. Remember that seeing a female figure in a dream represents the yang/masculine aspects of the dreamer's life; in this case, his thoughts and actions. Again, the white is congruent with the yang elements of the dream by its inherent male/yang associations.

14. Numbers

Numbers can play an important role in our dreams. Essentially, numbers are symbols that can represent both archetypal energies of the collective unconscious and personal associations. For example, Chinese people culturally consider the number 8 to be very auspicious so that a dream containing the archetypal number 8 will be read by a Chinese dreamer as a sign of good fortune. However, another individual may associate the number 8 to the house or street number where they lived when they were a child. Personal associations with numbers can signify the date an event took place or will take place like an anniversary or a birthday, an important hour related to a recent incident or memories, or even a personal "lucky number." Numbers may appear in a series or sequence, as stand-alone or repeating in sequence, or as in the number of objects in the dream, i.e. 2 apples. Patterns and repeating sequences in our dreams can reveal patterns that reoccur in our life.

The archetype number 0 represents the yin or feminine energy. The figure 0 itself represents the circle of life, returning to the source, continuation, wholeness, infinity and eternity, origin and completion. If you dream of the number one, it may imply masculine trends of your thoughts and actions in your waking life. We are also reminded that numbers 0 (yin) and 1 (yang) are used in the universal binary language of programming codes and algorithms in computers today. The number 3, also represented symbolically by a triangle, can be a metaphor for the Trinity. The number 4, suggested by the shape of a square, adds the archetypal symbol of the Madonna, an ultimate feminine energy. However, it is important to note that these numbers are not meant to be seen in a religious sense but rather imply the archetypal concept of spiritual completion. Numbers of male and female figures in a dream symbolize the preponderance of yin or yang energy in the dream. For example, a dream with 4 men and 2 women can be seen as an energetic preponderance of feminine yin energy in the dream, keeping in mind the anima and animus paradox.

To analyze numbers in dreams, again look at both archetypal and personal associations to help the dreamer give contextual meaning to the number appearing in the dream. If a non-integer number like 26 appears, investigate the meanings of both number 2 and number 6. For added insight, numerology suggests you add the digits together, reducing them to a single digit: in this case, eight. Then look at the meaning of the single digit eight. In a further example of personal associations to numbers, one person dreaming of the number 81 relates that to a significant year in their life, while another person associates the number to an airport gate they frequently used flying to a work destination.

15. Dream Case Studies

The dream itself is its own best interpretation.

- Carl Jung

I have selected these case studies because they contain important symbols that we find are common to many dreamers. Case studies have long been used in teaching when instructors want students to explore what they have learned as it applies to real-life situations. When you are learning to read dreams you will oftentimes come to an image or sequence in a dream that allows you to relate the language of the unconscious to waking life situations and circumstances. Dream case studies will give you some hands-on exposure as to how this process of analysis really works toward healing and balance.

Don, 62, Real Estate Businessman

I'm in a very large castle. I am working on some things.

"Working" means that Don is in his yang mode. "Castle" represents not only the physical business but the whole business, such as a corporation, i.e. his real estate business. That's where he is working on something "large" like a big business project. A castle is typically a symbol that indicates qualities such as stately, grand and important. It can refer to a family dynasty. Any dream where one is in a building represents a particular situation or circumstance where one finds oneself currently in their life.

> *Then I hear a sound, like a person down below who wants to open up the big castle door.*

When you are "down" or something is happening "down below" it means one is sensing something from their feeling-centeredness, the yin side.

> *Because there is someone there, I walk down the stone stairway.*

He senses a call from his gut or feeling-centered side and he is ready to further explore the situation.

> *I see a little girl pointing at the big door down below.*

"Little girl" represents some new thoughts or ideas (yang). "Big door" represents an important, potential transition, a new way through a situation or circumstance that the dreamer is in his waking life.

> *The big door has a smaller, lower door embedded in it. I open up the small lower section of the door.*

The "smaller, lower door" indicates that Don's unconscious is telling him to work through his project or situation, one section at a time.

> *I see another little girl is outside, beyond the door, who appears to be coming home from school.*

More ideas represented by the little girl, a yang symbol, are coming to him because he is learning something new. "School" is a symbol of where we learn new things or are presented with new ideas.

> *I turned around to have her hop on my shoulders.*

He is now owning these new ideas. Hopping on his shoulders indicates a lot of energy, he is energized by incorporating these new ideas.

> *Since it was a big step down to get to the big door, the first girl did not come down.*

His first impulse was to go down into his feelings (yin). However, this part of the dream means he is conflicted. The first girl symbol represents him wanting to stay "up" in his logic or head space to check out the situation logically.

> *But I ended up just talking to the other, little girl downstairs. They were both Asians.*

He is mulling around these new ideas. The Asian aspect means these new ideas are "foreign" to him.

Summation

Many times you will know the dreamer, or you will know yourself if you are reading your own dream. In this case, I know that Don has traveled in the Far East and he honors and respects Asian culture. Therefore, the Asian aspects mean that he is honoring these new ideas that are coming in through his dream in order for him to successfully get to the other side of the projects he is "working" on within the family business as represented by the castle symbol.

Joe, 29, Associate Professor

> *I am upstairs in my house.*

Being in a house upstairs means that he is in his head, the thinking mode (yang/male).

> *I am standing in the spot that the washing machine would normally be but it isn't there.*

The washing machine cleans one's personas, meaning one's outward presentation of oneself. He is having a hard time keeping up his persona.

> *There was another man there my age and he wasn't wearing anything except for his underwear.*

As every figure in the dream is an aspect of the dreamer's self, the other man depicts Joe's feelings/yin part. The man in his underwear indicates that Joe's feelings are exposed.

> *I don't think I was fully clothed myself.*

As both figures in the dream are not fully clothed, an indication of a doubling up or greater intensity of feelings is being bared.

> *He made a flirtatious advance toward me, reaching his hands for my butt, indicating he was gay.*

The man reaching for his butt means Joe's feelings are not upfront or overt yet but that they are wanting to be known. Joe is not yet ready to confront his feelings fully but his unconscious is pointing attention to certain feelings that want to be acknowledged.

> *I informed him that I wasn't gay and I didn't share the feeling that he apparently had for me.*

At this point, Joe assures himself that he is not gay. However, he is still not willing to confront some feelings in his life that can be further explored.

Note:

If a man dreams of any homosexual references this means he is operating primarily out of the feminine (yin) aspect at this time in his life, not from his logical male (yang) aspect. If a woman dreams of any lesbian references this means she is tempted to operate primarily out of her masculine (yang) aspect at the time of her dream, not from her feeling centeredness (yin) aspect. Therefore, having dreams wherein there are same-sex encounters does not necessarily denote one's sexual preferences.

The man immediately looked crestfallen but I also informed him that I knew a different guy who was also gay, and that he and this other guy would likely get along. This seemed to raise his spirit some.

Joe is trying to assuage his own feelings, trying to accept them but he is still deferring having to deal with his own feelings or trying to compartmentalize them.

I felt a little creepy.

Joe is feeling "creepy" or uncomfortable in being made aware or being exposed to his feminine (yin) feeling-centered side.

Summation:

Dreams that involve nudity or even partially-clothed persons indicate that the unconscious is talking about an individual's persona; their outward, everyday self. It can mean that the authentic self is exposed and present without the usual armor or shielding. Nudity dreams indicate either a confidence in exposing one's vulnerabilities, or if there is embarrassment or hiding of the nakedness it means the dreamer is uncomfortable in allowing himself or herself to be vulnerable and might want to pay attention to areas in their life where they are uneasy.

In this dream, Joe's unconscious is making him aware that his life-operating systems are out of balance. The dream alerts him to this imbalance. From my sessions with Joe the young professor, I realized that he was up in his head most of the time and a late bloomer in various areas of his life such as sexuality and romance. At the time, Joe was interested in a young lady and was having difficulties in creating a real relationship with her which made him feel more vulnerable and exposed.

Thomas, 67, Author

I was flying above some open desert space like Las Vegas. I was remote-controlling my car on the highway while I was flying about 20 feet high and positioning my car between 2 other moving cars.

Thomas is controlling, organizing his life from his head, his thinking-centeredness. The cars represent one's way through life. He is operating and strategizing more from an "open space," that is, a broad perspective rather than being actually integrated with the execution of his life.

I started gaining altitude and suddenly realized that I had lost contact with my car and couldn't descend down to it. I realized I was really high up about, 20 stories up and I knew that I was going to die if I fell.

He is going further into his idea-state rather than being in touch with the real world below. He loses connection with his way through life (symbolized by car). He has a fear that he will die if he comes down from his head into his feelings.

I decided I was not going to fall and somehow crawled through the air to a side of a tall building and clambered onto the balcony.

He does not want to get into his feelings (by falling down) so he is going to side-step his feelings by entering a building in order to avoid his feelings. The dream reader may ask at this point, "What are you trying to avoid feeling right now in your life?"

The balcony door was closed but then it opened and some wealthy family returned from a trip. Apparently, I was a servant there and I had to bow to some family members. The head of the family looked familiar but I couldn't make him out, maybe a young Bill Clinton.

He goes to a place where he can gather his thoughts and feelings, as depicted by male and female family members. He is facing some sort of familiar life script of being undeserving depicted by his servile bowing. I asked Thomas how he viewed Bill Clinton as a character type. Thomas indicated that Clinton represents a shady character. That tells us of Thomas's distrust of his own inner feelings (yin).

> *Then a female pianist from my church started playing piano in the room and there were some boys and girls around and a nice feeling of fun, and singing.*

Now Thomas is starting to get some new, emerging thoughts and feelings as represented by the kids. Also, those new, emerging thoughts and feelings are coming from a new place, not a familiar place, rather a spiritual place represented by the church music.

Summation:

Dreams in which an individual is flying represent a dreamer who is observing matters or working out problems from a headspace, one's thinking-centered or logical (yang) side. Being grounded is a yin/feminine feeling aspect whereas flying can indicate the opposite; that is, avoiding feelings. I know that Thomas was beginning a romantic relationship during this time after a long period of bachelorhood. This dream indicates his uncertainty and fear of falling down into his feelings, and his tendency to stay in his intellectual self and his old familiar (or familial) script. Being a writer, this is Thomas's more habitual way of handling life.

Dylan, 20, Student

> *I was waiting to enter a public bath very much like the ones in Japan with mostly men there except it was located on some kind of large campus with a river running through it. I saw a small tan young girl with long black hair.*

The dream location is on a campus which is a nature setting with a river, so Dylan is moving toward his sensuality as represented by the symbol of the river water. The campus represents a place of learning, expanding consciousness and thinking (yang attributes). The bath, again a water symbol, represents sensuality. There are mostly men, with some women. So, Dylan is having both thoughts and feelings in the area of sexuality/sensuality.

> *The young girl was wearing a somewhat tight two-piece bathing suit, and she greatly resembled Lilo, the cartoon character from the Disney movie "Lilo and Stitch." For some reason, I got turned on by her. I had a desire to see that girl naked.*

The small girl with black hair and the swimsuit is cartoonish. Upon questioning Dylan, he revealed his association related to Lilo as an independent, mischievous and eccentric character. It is his own emerging manhood that is being represented here in a juvenile way, depicted by the cartoonish young girl. Remember that the female figure always represents a yang, masculine aspect of the dreamer.

> *I entered the public bath with this group of people with my clothes and other stuff in hand. They had already gotten undressed and were in the water and I noticed the girl had no clothes on. I perversely glanced in her direction though it seemed I couldn't get a good look. Then, oddly, several of the men in that group wouldn't let me into the water.*

He was naked, meaning he has shed his outer persona, preparing himself physically for a relationship. Entering the bath and seeing the naked girl says he is preparing himself mentally for sensuality, as depicted by the girl symbol which is his male, thinking side. The other men who do not allow his entry into the water represent his feelings of trepidation that are holding him back from pursuing a relationship. Again, male figures in the dream represent our feelings.

> *The men suddenly spoke harshly, forcing me to leave the public bath. I felt angry. I somehow acquired a wet wad of toilet paper and threw it hard in their direction. It landed on the wall. Then one of the men got out of the water looking rather pissed off. The look in his eyes was alarming.*

He threw wet toilet paper at them demonstrating his own adolescent behavior. The image of wet toilet paper (not exactly a weapon) represents a weak response or defense against his strong negative feelings.

> *Sensing danger, I promptly ran for it. I dashed down a hallway, making a left. The man was not far behind me and had somehow gotten his clothes back on. I was no longer carrying my clothes around, I was now wearing them. I sprinted, making another left. This was seemingly a dead end.*

His feelings are taking over now but he is running away from them. He is starting to shut down his vulnerability by putting his clothes back on. Left turns represent turning toward one's feminine (yin) receptive side.

> *I had to face the man. He had me cornered now. Then he took out a knife. This man had every intention to kill me. I had nothing. No weapon with which to defend myself. Then he threw the knife at me.*

Dylan is being overwhelmed by his feelings here as represented by the man confronting him, as every image in the dream is always another aspect of ourself. The knife, I explain to him, is a phallic symbol. The knife being thrown at him represents his intense fear of his own male sexuality.

> *Thankfully the knife missed me. I think I may have even caught the knife. Regardless, I acquired the knife. The man seemed troubled but still intent on doing me harm. I swung the knife at him and he attempted to dodge. I'm fairly certain that I struck him once or twice and I believe there was blood*

Dylan doesn't know how to handle his own sexuality as symbolized by the chaotic knife (phallic symbol) interactions. He now has the knife which represents his struggle with his sexuality. There was blood, meaning that this whole conflict with his manhood and his sexuality feels life-threatening.

> *Then more trouble. A man who worked on the campus was heading down the hallway in our direction. The man that attacked me attempted to draw attention to the knife which I now held in my hand in order to place blame on me.*

Indicating "blame" means Dylan has some feelings of guilt, compounding his feelings of sexual anxiety.

> *However, I stealthily hid the knife from sight and the worker didn't notice. The attacking man's wounds were unnoticed by the worker. The worker thought it was nonsense for me to have a knife. Then I don't know what happened to the man that attacked me but he seemed to vanish into thin air. The worker gestured for me to come to him. He then showed*

me an enormous display of foreign cultural objects that I had either not noticed or it simply hadn't been there until that very moment.

"Hiding" the knife represents a retreating back into adolescence. That's like retracting his sexuality. However, the worker symbol is a constructive, positive feeling within Dylan that there is a new and different way of dealing with this issue as represented by the symbols of "foreign culture."

Summation

In a death dream, there is a letting go of, or a preparing of the dreamer for some kind of loss whether it be a loss of a person or a situation in life. This type of dream prepares one for a transformation and oftentimes involves violence. The old has to die for the new to be born. The dreamer may be at a breaking point over something in their waking life. There may be a person, circumstance or even some deep internal need to exert an emotional catharsis. Sometimes the death dream can lead the dreamer to change their own self-defeating behaviors, thereby expanding their personal, social and spiritual development.

There are PTSD dreams wherein violence is played out as a memory or as an allegory of a distressful memory. Some death dreams about fighting or killing can represent the process of being physically sick when cells are battling it out for the dreamer to get well. Reading a dream of violence does not mean that the dreamer is violent in their waking life or is considering a violent act. Contacts with the dead may also take place in dreams. The human psyche does indeed go beyond time and space via the unconscious through dreams.

From previous sessions with Dylan, I was aware that he was a virgin just starting to explore his sexuality, along with an interest in having a relationship with a female student friend. The violence aspect of the dream is an example of the unconscious drawing very forceful attention even to the point of knives and blood that Dylan the dreamer is ready to aggressively move past his juvenile behavior patterns and fearful feelings. This dream helped him to better understand his inner turmoil and his fears in moving forward toward sexual and relationship maturity.

Ann, 46, Personal Assistant

> *I have a Samurai sword. I am stabbing the abdomen of a middle-aged man, trying to kill him. Striking in a downward motion, then down and over to the right to make sure that it severed the guts inside.*

Upon questioning Ann on her association with a samurai sword, she lets me know that this kind of sword represents the highest or most noble attributes related to the honor, skill and courage of a samurai. A sword, I inform Ann, represents a masculine phallic (yang) energy. By stabbing the abdomen of a middle-aged man, representing a current feeling (same age as Ann), the dream tells us that she wants to eviscerate a feeling (male figure representing feelings), a feeling that she no longer wants, to completely obliterate or destroy that feeling cognitively (again male-thinking energy). Cutting down and across to the right indicates the skillful, expert manner of the samurai method of *hara-kiri* (suicide). She wants to completely "sever the guts" meaning to get rid of this no-longer-needed feeling on a visceral level yet in a manner of complete integrity.

Summation

Many times people use alcohol or drugs to hide their feelings or circumstances. Here the dreamer is using a completely cognizant, rational methodology to deal with a particular situation in her life. Knowing Ann, I can see that her unconscious is reflecting her waking life where she is in a process of letting go of people and circumstances that cause her pain and that no longer serve her. Ann said she felt a deep sense of resolve from this dream. So, you can see that even though on the surface this dream appears to be about death, the dream is really about a transformative process of eliminating the old, thus creating new space so that more positive energy can come into her life.

Linda, 42, Healthcare Professional.

I was in my living room observing a cat on a couch. The cat seemed like it was sucked in, panting and dying of dehydration or maybe of cancer, or something else.

The cat, I inform Linda, is a yin image representing the feminine. The living room is in Linda's house. That location describes where one is at emotionally at this time of their life, i.e. your current state of being, also referred to as a "status quo" dream. The cat being "sucked in" or "dehydrated" indicates that it is without fluids or lack of nutrients, kind of a husk of itself as if the life was being sucked out of it. The lack of fluids, i.e. water, indicates the extreme lack of sensuality and sexuality in the dreamer's waking life.

Those aspects of Linda's life are being neglected or not being nurtured.

Summation

Illness dreams are bringing the dreamer's attention to physical, mental, emotional and spiritual needs that want to be addressed or tended to in order for the dreamer to get on a path of well-being. There may be a warning of some serious damage to one's health that the unconscious knows of before an individual becomes aware of the actual symptoms in their waking life. Illness dreams symbolize dangers, annoyances and inconveniences, some obstacles or delays, unfavorable circumstances, turmoil and difficulties, or even some ill-advised temptations.

Remember that the feminine (yin) dream image always represents the physical side of the dreamer. Also, note that a short dream can be just as significant as a longer, more complex narrative. I knew that Linda was currently struggling in a relationship that was non-sexual nor sensual but that she did have her material needs met from this relationship. The dream let her know that her innate femininity was dying from lack of true love, sensuality and affection.

Robin, 60, Business Owner

I was in a ladies' lounge. I was naked and two other ladies there, my same age, remarked on my beautiful breasts.

Being naked is a dropping of the persona, the individual's outward presentation. Linda agrees with me that breasts are an important symbol of the female as manifested in the physical form of femininity. "Ladies" or female figures in the dream represent the dreamer's mental (yang) side meaning her unconscious is making an analytical assessment. Mentioning the "same age" means the dream is depicting the dreamer's current ideas. A lounge is a place where thoughts and ideas are shared.

They ask me how is it that at my age I have such nice breasts? And I said you too could have nice breasts.

Referring to her age means how far she has come in life to date. "You too can have nice breasts" means that she is sounding back to herself that all is possible, that she is worthy of having the best in life, saying yes to herself, being affirmative.

> *"Yes, but how do they feel," they asked? I said, "See for yourself." Each one separately squeezed my breasts to see how they felt.*

The dreamer is reassessing and reaffirming her self-worth.

> *They said 'Wow!' They said that my breasts felt real. And I said, "See, they are super real, better than real, beyond real." They marveled and said, "You are right, Wow!"*

Now she is again reaffirming the positive aspects she determined previously relating to all the personal maturity she has evolved to at this point in her life and recognizing that she is in great shape physically, emotionally, mentally and spiritually.

> *I became happy with myself and happy that I could share something of myself with the other ladies.*

This last part indicates that she is fully embracing herself, "sharing" or integrating all the parts of herself in a holistic way.

Summation

Sexual body parts, whether the dreamer is male or female, relate to the dreamer's yin or yang aspects within themself. A penis, breasts or vagina appearing in a dream can connote a feeling of exposure and invasion of privacy. Breasts (yin) appearing in a dream can symbolize primal feminine attributes such as feelings and receptivity. A penis (yang) symbolizes potency and masculine attributes like thinking, action and business matters. The unconscious often calls attention to the dreamer's masculine potency or feminine receptivity in life through symbols related to sexual body parts

This dream is an evaluation dream, and an evaluation is a thinking-centered (yang) action. The breasts as a body parts symbol are relating to Robin's femininity. The dreamer is making a current adult evaluation of her authentic feminine identity, meaning that she has achieved a great degree of self-actualization in her life. She is pleased with how far she has come to date and she expresses her healthy self-esteem. From knowing Robin's history and her trajectory through therapy and personal growth classes, the dream is a validation of all the hard work she has done on herself.

Chloe, 8-year-old

I keep having this dream over and over. I am running away from an old, ugly, scary witch. She has old tattered clothes, a broom, scraggly hair, warts all over her face.

Chloe is having a recurring dream. This means that there is an unresolved issue in the dreamer's life. "Running away" means that the dreamer is afraid of confronting this issue. The "old, ugly, scary witch" is a classic witch female figure representing old scary thoughts and ideas. The "old tattered clothes" refer to an old persona. The broom is a phallic symbol.

I am flying by swimming in the air to get away from her. I am flying a few feet off the ground, just out of reach of the witch grabbing me, just ahead of her a little bit, swimming and flying as hard and fast as I can in order to get away, breathing really hard.

Chloe retreats to her male (yang) side in order to avoid her feelings by the symbolic flying or going up, representing an attempt to think her way out of what is hidden in her unconscious. She can't get enough height and speed in order to make her escape. That indicates she is desperately trying to go up into her thoughts (yang) in order to escape her scary feelings (yin).

The witch can't get to me even though she is also flying just below me, chasing me with her broom sticking out in front of her.

Again there is the "broom sticking out in front of her" as a phallic symbol. And again, she is trying to get away from a sexual trauma by flying up into her head (yang) and escaping her feelings (yin) which are "just below" her.

Summation

A repetitive, recurring dream derives from an unresolved issue where the unconscious is calling for a resolution. An unresolved issue need not always be depicted in a scary way but the terrifying monster factor (in this case, a witch) indicates the traumatic nature of this unresolved issue. Monster dreams usually contain scary images representing overwhelming, unresolved thoughts and feelings. Even though a monster dream may be deemed a nightmare, the unconscious is calling attention to someone or something important that the dreamer is dealing with or not dealing with, or that they don't understand. Even though monsters can come in multiple forms, remember that the aggressive and scary aspects of the monster indicate real and sizeable fears. Is there someone or something that is getting out of control in the dreamer's life? Maybe a situation has become an over-sized problem. Is the dreamer shocked by someone's actions in their life, or by someone who acts monstrously?

I know that Chloe was kidnapped and threatened with a sexual act at 5 years of age by a man. She managed to escape her abductor by hearing a saving voice in her head (thinking/yang faculty) that facilitated her escape. The dream shows that Chloe is plagued by the scary thoughts of a masculine phallic symbol chasing her, referring to the repressed trauma. She is repetitively running away from the scary thoughts about the sexual trauma that needs to be resolved. Chloe became ego-dystonic meaning that she stopped being grounded in her feminine as a result of this trauma. The goal is to help her through follow-up counseling in order for her to return to being grounded in her feminine (yin) feeling-centeredness.

We should remember that if there is no witch or dragon to face in a classic fairy tale or in our dream, there cannot be a heroic story. Without a negative element to overcome, there would be nothing to produce a heroic act and therefore there would be no development in one's personal life journey. Witch-ness and dragon-ness should be recognized as qualities which do exist in everyone's life. Without challenges in dreams or in our life, no personal evolution can take place.

There are no bad dreams, just scary images

– Dr. Pat Allen

Catherine, 36, Artist

I was floating upright in the ocean, not far from the shore, just up to my chest in the water, kind of moving with the ebb and flow of the tide. I was still able to touch the sandy bottom with my feet from time to time. I was enjoying the moment.

The dreamer is in an ocean, showing that she is already processing her romantic life, not just on the shore contemplating it. She is comfortable and enjoying where she is at in this area, at the present moment. The fact that her feet can touch the bottom indicates that she feels some measure of control, being grounded.

> *Suddenly, I felt an underwater surge and realized that a giant wave was coming toward me.*

The surge she feels represents a shift happening beneath her and represents her unknown and greater libidinous energies.

> *In a split second, I had to make a decision as to what I was going to do. I thought of getting away from the wave by heading back to the shore.*

At first, she feels afraid because of these new, unexpected feelings, so she wants to escape them, indicating that she wants to get away from the relationship.

> *Then I decided to turn and move head-on into the oncoming wave and dive down into it, thus allowing myself to be fully engulfed by the wave.*

Instead, she decides to turn toward the wave, indicating that she is willing to confront her fears. By fully submerging into the water, she is releasing her control and ready to surrender to a sensual/sexual relationship in her life.

Summation

Water dreams relate to sensual, sexual, or relationship issues in the dreamer's life. Specific water images indicate the level of intensity that the dreamer is experiencing, from a waterfall to an ocean to an ice cube. For example, a frozen pond image points to a relationship that is stuck, not flowing nor fluid. A bucolic flowing river suggests a relationship that is moving and healthy.

Working in dream sessions with Catherine I knew that she had recently met a man that she was attracted to after a long period of not being involved in any romantic relationships. She was adjusting to feeling comfortable and safe in this new romance, hoping not to sabotage it. The dream told her that she is ready to go deeper into the relationship, even to a point beyond her normal sense of control, though she did not acknowledge that consciously in her waking life. Diving into the big wave, instead of running from it, her unconscious through the dream was telling Catherine that she was indeed ready to surrender, to go fearlessly and deeper into this new romantic relationship.

Jacob, 44, Engineer

> *I bought an old, huge 1960's Lincoln in beautiful condition from a guy who looked like a drug addict or drug dealer. I drove the car around my old Bronx neighborhood (where I grew up until I left at age 18).*

Upon questioning Jacob regarding his associations with the old beautiful car, he reveals to me that he had owned these types of cars in the past. The dreamer is driving an old vehicle in his old neighborhood indicating metaphorically that he is doing things in his life in an old familiar pattern. Because the drug dealer is a male he represents the dreamer's (yin) feminine feeling side. In reading this dream I ask Jacob, "What feeling does a drug addict or drug dealer bring up for you?" In Jacob's particular dream, this symbol indicates negative feelings of distrust and suspicion showing that the dreamer is colluding with his own negative feelings about his way through life as represented by the old car.

> *Then I parked the car and got out. I tried to restart it again by using a kind of outside remote key starter but the car wouldn't start.*

He stops to reflect for a moment. He wants to resume ("restart") the old way of doing things but it doesn't work. He tries using a different tactic, i.e. the remote starter but his old ways just aren't working for him anymore.

> *I popped the hood. Inside the engine looked very simple but there was red fluid coming out of a part, like transmission fluid.*

Jacob is starting to reflect inside himself, to do some inner work. This inner view looks simple at first. The red transmission fluid symbolizes his lifeblood. The root chakra is red, representing the basic survival instinct. This means there is something very basic that has caused him to stop as his unconscious recognizes that he is bleeding figuratively on the inside.

> *I asked the drug dealer guy about buying parts and he said, "It could be a few weeks."*

He is still trying to piece his old ways back together.

> *Then he said, "Personally, I think you're crazy to have bought it." Then he said, "I'll have to get you a 1001 form to fill out."*

At this point, Jacob is sensing on a feeling level that it is crazy to buy into this old way. A form is a bureaucratic way of doing something which always connotes a slow and cumbersome system. He now wants to get out of his survival mode but his feelings are holding him back.

> *I was really distressed about the $5000 I had paid for the car. I was going to call Jim (my former business partner) to see if he could help me.*

The dreamer is really distressed about how much he has invested in his old trusted ways. He is now turning toward listening to his trusted gut feelings, depicted by his business partner.

> *Then I realized that I hadn't actually given the guy any money, and I said to myself, "Fuck it, I'm not going to pay the guy."*

Now he has an '*aha moment*' in the dream. The dream is telling Jacob that he is ready to take control and move in a new direction.

Summation

From what Jacob has shared previously with me in sessions, I know that he is going through a midlife crisis. He is coming to a point in his life where he realizes that the old ways in which he operated no longer work for him. The dream is telling him that he can forcefully or definitively end that deep-rooted mode of moving through his life, allowing himself to seek new and more effective behaviors. Through the dream work we are doing together Jacob is starting to connect the dots about specific patterns and doing some inner work which allows for these types of *aha moments* to come up in his dreams. Note that this is an example of the beginnings of rational decision-making that can be sparked by dream work.

Final Thoughts

Tibetan monks train in ancient dreaming techniques because they see the dream state, the waking state, the deep sleep state and the *bardo* (the state between death and rebirth) as the places where we all live individually and collectively at different times within the entire unified field of mind and matter. One of their practices is to stop during one's daily life and look around your surroundings and within yourself as if you are experiencing a dream. This exercise helps in developing mindfulness, and mindfulness is the key to understanding what is happening to us in the present moment, as well as in what the mystics call *the timeless moment.*

My hope is that once you have absorbed the teachings presented in *The Dream Class* you will develop greater mindfulness through using the techniques of capturing your dreams, reading the symbols more accurately and applying the lessons the unconscious generously gives to us. In this way, we can begin to live a more balanced and fruitful life in this ever-increasing complicated place we inhabit together today. There are more dream circles and associations today as well as more qualified dream guides available since many of us are looking for deeper answers to the mysteries of life. May your dream journeys bring you greater awareness to what the Universe has to offer you!

Recommended Books

Dream Analysis, Carl Jung (Princeton University Press)

Animus and Anima, Emma Jung (Spring Publications)

Dreams and Healing, John A. Sanford (Paulist Press)

Heal Your Body A – Z, Louise L. Hay (Hay House)

It's a Man's World and a Woman's Universe, Patricia Allen (Balboa Press)

Yin and Yang of Life, Joseph K. Kim and David S. Lee (Heal and Soul)

Transactional Analysis in Psychotherapy, Eric Berne (Castle Books)

Mysterium Coniunctionis, Carl Jung, Princeton University Press

Toward a Psychology of Being, Abraham Maslow (Van Nostrand Reinhold)

Love on the Brain, Daniel Amen (Three Rivers Press)

The Mystical Magical Marvelous World of Dreams, Wilda B. Tanner (Sparrow Hawk Press)

What is Dreaming?, Etan Boritzer (Veronica Lane Books)

He/She/We, Robert A. Johnson (Harper)

Jungian Dream Interpretation, James A. Hall (Inner City Books)

Subliminal: How Your Unconscious Mind Rules Your Behavior, Leonard Mlodinow (Vintage Press)

Dreaming – Journal of the International Association for the Study of Dreams, (Educational Publishing Foundation of the American Psychological Association)

Index

Age-related dreams, 52

Aha moment, iii

Allen, Dr. Pat, vii, 1, 7, 11, 13, 14, 22, 75
    dream readings, viii

Alzheimer's disease, 2

Analytical psychology, 13

Androgynous, 13

Androgynous Semantic Realignment (ASR), 14, 22

Anima, 13
    expression of, 22
    in waking state, 24
    unconscious, 24

Animus, 13
    expression of, 22
    woman's innate animus masculine/yang side, 23

Archetypes, 13
    symbol of Madonna, 75

Articles, in dreams, 52

Asian cultures
    black color, significance of, 71
    numbers, significance of, 75
    white color, significance of, 73

Awakening of insights, 4

Bardo state, 99

Berne, Eric, 17

Black color, 71–72

Black Madonna, 71

Body-related dreams, 52

Building-related dreams, 53

Case studies
    Ann, 88–89
    Catherine, 94–96
    Chloe, 92–94
    Don, 77–79
    Dylan, 84–88
    Jacob, 96–98
    Joe, 79–81
    Robin, 90–92
    Thomas, 82–83

Chakras, 60, 61
    arrangement of, 63
    crown (*Sahasrara*), 70
    heart (*Anahata*), 67
    root (*Muladhara*), 64
    sacral (*Swadhisthana*), 65

solar plexus (*Manipura*), 66

theory of, 62

third eye (*Ajna*), 69

throat (*Vishuddhi*), 68

Clothing-related dreams, 53

Collective Unconscious, 14

Color-related dreams, 54, 60–61

black objects, 71–72

chakras as color symbol, 62

subjective and personal associations of, 60

white objects, 73–74

Consciousness, 14

Crown chakra (*Sahasrara*), 70

Daily-life dreams, 8

Death, as dream theme, 41

Desensitization, 14, 36

Dream reader, 31, 34

Dream readings, viii, 31–32

anima/animus paradox, 38

archetypes, interpreting, 39

as a tool, 31

interpreting symbols, 34–37

process of, 33–40

yin/yang of dreams, 37

Dream symbols. *See* Symbols of dream

Dream themes

death, 41

drugs and drinking, 41

examinations, 42

falling, 42

flying, 43

lost, 43

money, 43

nudity, 44

pregnancy, 44

sex, 44–45

war, 45

Dreams

as an emotional convalescence, 2

as coded version of inner workings of mind, 1

capturing of, 26–30

definition, 1

for self-discovery and problem-solving, 1

interpretation in Western culture, 3

rationale for, 4–7

sources of, 3

Dreams, types of

about past, 8–9

daliy-life dreams, 8

lucid dreams, 11–12

prophetic or predictive dreams, 9–10
pruning dreams, 10
trauma dreams, 10–11
Drinking, as dream theme, 41
Drugs, as dream theme, 41
Ego, 14
Ego-dystonic, 14
Ego-syntonic, 15
Emotional stability, dreams and, 5–6
Emotionally-charged dream images. See Nightmares
Examinations, as dream theme, 42
Extra-sensory perception (ESP), 9
Falling dreams, 42
Feminine (yin) energy, viii, See also Yin Yang
general characteristics of, 21
Flying dreams, 43
Food and drink, in dreams, 55
Furniture-related dreams, 55
Healing business, vi
Heart *chakra* (*Anahata*), 67
Individuation, 15
Instinct, 15, 24, 27
Intuition, 4, 15, 23, 27
Isis (goddess), 71
Jung, Carl, 1, 13, 17, 22, 25

Kala (Sanskrit), 71
Kali (goddess), 71
Language of dreaming mind, 1
Life Script, 15
Limen state, 15
capturing dreams in, 26–30
Locales, in dreams, 56
Lost, as dream theme, 43
Lucid dreams, 11–12
Masculine (*yang*) energy, viii, See also Yin Yang
general characteristics of, 21
Maslow, Abraham, 17
Memory consolidation, 10
Memory pruning, 10
Metaphor, 15
Money dreams, 43
Mythological figures, as dreams, 56–57
Myths, 16
Nadis, 62
Nightmares, 2, 5, 12
NREM dreaming, 2
Nudity dreams, 44
Numbers, in dreams, 75–76
Past (daily events), dreams about, 8–9
People-related dreams, 57

Persona, 16
Precognitive dream, vi
Pregnancy dreams, 44
Prophetic or predictive dreams, 9–10
Psyche, 16
Psychoanalysis, 16
Quality of life, dreams and, 4–5
Rapid eye movement (REM) sleep cycle, 2
Rational decision making, 16
Relationships, dreams and, 5
REM dreaming, 2
Repression, 16
Root *chakra* (*Muladhara*), 64
Sacral *chakra* (*Swadhisthana*), 65
Seeker, v
Self, 16
Self-actualization, 17
Sex-related dreams, 44–45
Shadow, 17
Shaman, 32
Solar plexus *chakra* (*Manipura*), 66
Sports/games-related dreams, 54
Stress/anxiety reflief, dreams and, 6
Subconscious, 17
Suppression, 17

Symbol, 17
Symbols of dream, 46–50, *See also* Color-related dreams
  age, 52
  articles, 52
  body and bodily health, 52
  buildings, 53
  clothing, 53
  colors, 54
  food and drink, 55
  furniture, 55
  games, 54
  locales, 56
  mythological figures, 56–57
  nature, 49
  people, 49, 57
  teeth, 58
  things, 50
  trees, 58
  underwater creatures, 58
  vehicles, 59
  water, 59
Syndrome, 17
Tabula rasa, 73
Taijitu symbol, 20, 23, 73
Teeth-related dreams, 58

Third eye *chakra* (*Ajna*), 69

Throat chakra (*Vishuddhi*), 68

Tibetan monks, 99

Timeless moment, 99

Transactional analysis, 17

Trauma dreams, 10–11

Trees-related dreams, 58

Unconscious, 18
- anima, 24
- animus, 24
- mind, 1, 2, 13, 14, 22, 57
- referencing of sensual/sexual relationship, 56

Underwater creatures-related dreams, 58

Vehicle-related dreams, 59

WANT® Institute, Orange County, vii

War-related dreams, 45

Water-related dreams, 59

White color, 73–74

White dove, symbolic meaning of, 73

Yin Yang, 18, 23
- dualities in, 18, 19–20
- effect of interplay of yin and yang, 20
- feminine characteristics of, 21
- masculine characteristics of, 21
- meaning, 19
- symbol, 20

Yoga, 62

www.ingramcontent.com/pod-product-compliance
Lightning Source LLC
Chambersburg PA
CBHW061119070526
44583CB00028B/3336